UPCYC
SHELTE
WORKSH PS

UPCYCLING SHELTERED WORKSHOPS

A REVOLUTIONARY APPROACH FOR TRANSFORMING WORKSHOPS INTO CREATIVE SPACES

Susan Dlouhy and Patty Mitchell

Foreword by Lynn M. Harter

SWALLOW PRESS
OHIO UNIVERSITY PRESS
Athens

Swallow Press
An imprint of Ohio University Press, Athens, Ohio 45701
ohioswallow.com

Printed in the United States of America
Swallow Press / Ohio University Press books are printed on acid-free paper ∞ ™

25 24 23 22 21 20 19 18 17 16 15 5 4 3 2 1

Library of Congress Cataloging-in-Publication Data
Dlouhy, Susan, author.
Upcycling sheltered workshops : a revolutionary approach for transforming workshops into creative spaces / Susan Dlouhy and Patty Mitchell ; foreword by Lynn M. Harter.
p. ; cm.
ISBN 978-0-8040-1159-4 (pb : alk. paper) — ISBN 978-0-8040-4063-1 (pdf)
I. Mitchell, Patty, 1965 May 2– , author. II. Title.
[DNLM: 1. Sheltered Workshops—United States. 2. Creativity—United States. 3. Developmental Disabilities—rehabilitation—United States. 4. Intellectual Disability—rehabilitation—United States. 5. Models, Educational—United States. WM 29 AA1]
HV1553
362.4'04848—dc23
2014044058

Dedicated to our many friends with challenges, who have shown us that with the right support and encouragement they can do brilliant things and bring light and joy to their communities. You have created the evidence for this book and encouraged others to imagine and make a richer environment for the human spirit to soar.

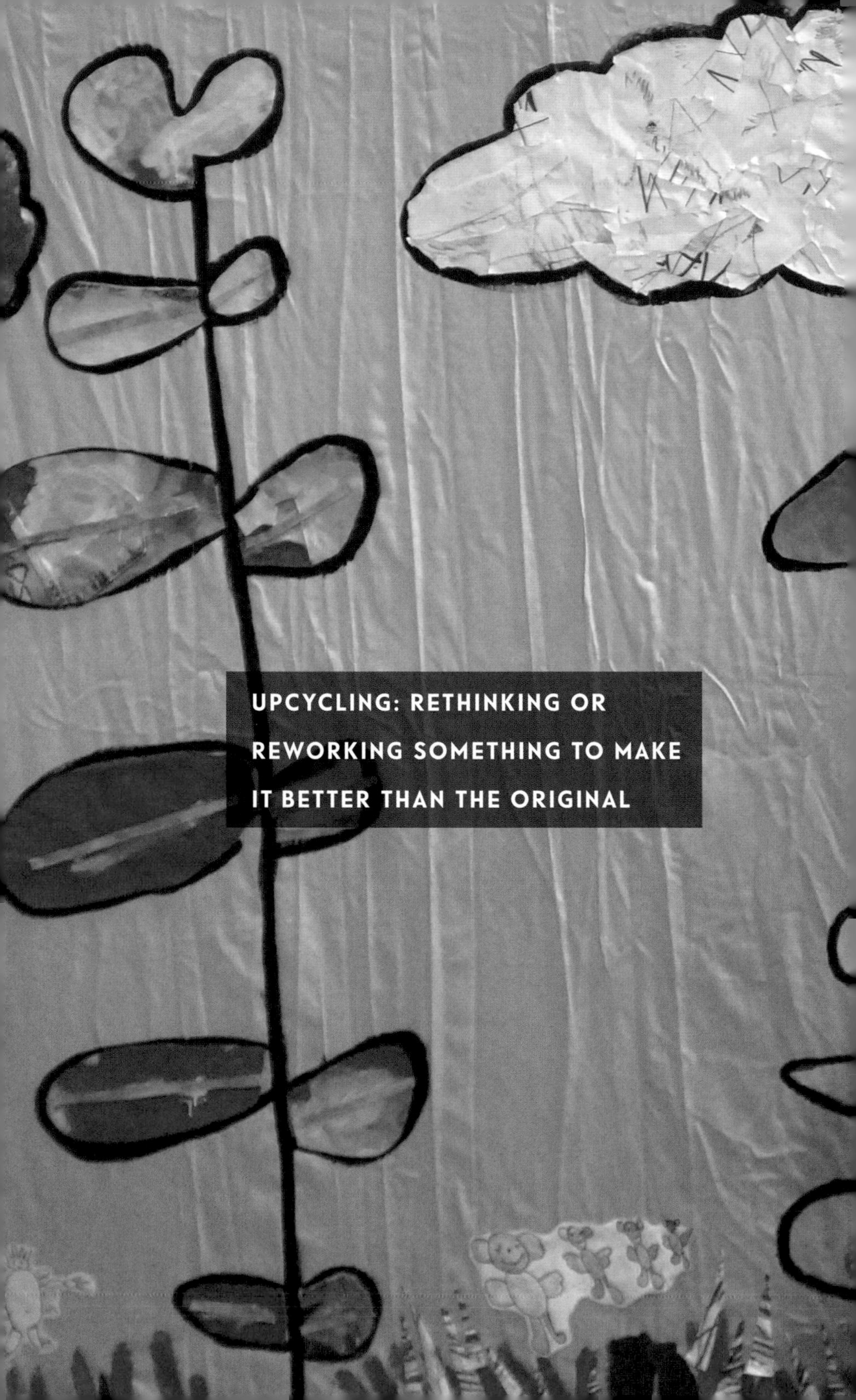

UPCYCLING: RETHINKING OR REWORKING SOMETHING TO MAKE IT BETTER THAN THE ORIGINAL

ONCE YOU LABEL ME YOU NEGATE ME
—Sören Kierkegaard

contents

Elizabeth and Dr. Lynn Harter working in the Up and Beyond Art Studio, Highland County, Ohio.

(UP AND BEYOND ART STUDIO, HILLSBORO, OHIO)

foreword

SHELTERED WORKSHOPS ACROSS the United States offer vocational and rehabilitative services for individuals with intellectual and developmental disabilities. These workshops are populated with well-intentioned staff, individuals who coordinate resources, including employment opportunities, for the people they serve. Production specialists organize facility-based employment, while other staff members arrange integrated, community-based employment. Over the past ten years, however, prospects for facility-based work have declined, and the supply of integrated employment opportunities has not kept pace with demand. In short, the system is broken. Policy makers and citizens alike must confront a pressing societal dilemma: the need to create expressive and vocational opportunities for people with intellectual and developmental disabilities. In this volume, Susan Dlouhy and Patty Mitchell offer a revolutionary and compelling solution to the sheltered workshop problem—the Creative Abundance Model.

Dlouhy and Mitchell begin with an appreciative stance toward people, organizations, and communities. Despite frequent and earnest discussions of putting the principles of self-determination and thinking ability first, the provision of services in sheltered workshops continues to be organized around people's limitations. Deficit-oriented models focus on shortcomings and envision resources as scarce. As a result, program design can limit people by inadvertently positioning them as bundles of pathologies or problems to be fixed. The Creative Abundance Model shifts the focus to people's interests and capacities. Dlouhy and Mitchell recognize and accept fallibility and vulnerability as part of the human condition; however, they position people's gifts as more powerful than their deficiencies or needs.

The Creative Abundance Model envisions workshops as spaces for creative activity. An artistic mindset is central to helping staff members break away from preconceived ways of seeing things. Rather than correcting or curing perceived imperfections, staff members help individuals identify and explore their interests. Starting from an appreciative standpoint, staff members provide resources and support for individuals to develop previously untapped gifts. Whether the staff elevates a table to accommodate wheelchairs, engages in conversations about the medium artists would like to work with, stirs paints, or cleans brushes, they do so with the intent of helping others follow their creative impulses and express themselves.

Participating artists are intrinsically rewarded by opportunities for self-expression. Just as important, though, is that artful practices provide a scaffold for achieving other goals, such as paid labor—and there is great dignity in being paid for one's artwork. Drawing on years of experience, Dlouhy and Mitchell illustrate how workshops can embrace art as both creation (that is, process) and vocation (that is, product). In studios, products spring from artful expressions that gain consumers' attention—sculptures, drawings, images, patterns, and collages. As products enter the marketplace, artists receive monetary compensation for their creativity. In sum, as illustrated throughout this volume, art represents a mechanism for both expression and employment. As such, art allows participants to become more fully integrated in community life.

I am optimistic that this book will help readers revolutionize how workshops serve their constituents. No project is ever complete or final. Even so, the Creative Abundance Model is a starting point for fostering progressive change. Dlouhy and Mitchell offer a set of practices worthy of modeling, and they encourage readers to imagine a future beyond the familiar. Envisioning alternative possibilities is the first step in shaping a more fulfilling social order.

Lynn M. Harter

Barbara Geralds Schoonover Professor of Health Communication,
Scripps College of Communication

preface

PEOPLE ARE PEOPLE. People with cognitive challenges, however, are continually being labeled and relabeled. Everyone is weighing in: administrators, self-advocacy groups, family members, accreditation bodies, the federal government, and state agencies. Terms such as *clients, consumers, employees, enrollees, individuals, individuals receiving services, people with perceived intellectual disabilities,* and *persons served* all tend to separate us. Look up *people* in a thesaurus, and you will see an infinite list of possible labels, most of which we are using or have used in the past. Recently, other labels such as *member* and *associate* have surfaced. These terms would be fine if everyone in the

Juliana Thomas and artist Angel Vruno working on a portrait of Marilyn Monroe.
(CREATIVE FOUNDATIONS, MOUNT VERNON, OHIO)

building shared the same label. But they don't. The staff members have labels that define them as being somehow different: *support specialist, workshop supervisor, program specialist, habilitation specialist, direct care worker, vocational trainer.*

Each of us at different times has a label that helps define who we are in certain situations. How is it that we can be patients, employees, clients, customers, and consumers without those labels having a negative connotation? It seems, however, that any terminology that we use to describe someone who has perceived differences becomes a negative. We are not attempting to resolve this historic debate, but we are going to make a conscious effort to refer to people as just *people* (and maybe *folks,* at times). The occasional reference to disability or difference may be necessary to provide context.

acknowledgments

THANK YOU to the Ohio Arts Council, whose Artist in Residence and other programs supported the necessary original experiences of developing art studios within sheltered workshops. Thank you to Melanie Stretchbery, Stacy Collins, Jordan Freeze, Andria Kleiner, and Terri O'Connell for being our volunteer content editors; and to Robert Lockheed and Barb Seckler for being our supportive partners and biggest fans. We couldn't have done it without your love, kindness, and generosity. And we definitely couldn't have done it without our original support system, our parents, Peg and Joe Dlouhy and Mimi and Bob Mitchell.

UPCYCLING SHELTERED WORKSHOPS

Sheltered workshops are typically housed in large communal spaces.

Turning workshops into creative community spaces changes the vibe. Painter Nancy, working her magic at the WASCO sheltered workshop. WASCO also has a studio in downtown Marietta, Ohio, called Heart to Art Galleria, where individuals make and sell their artwork. (WASCO, MARIETTA, OHIO)

1 THE MOVEMENT TOWARD THE CREATIVE ABUNDANCE MODEL

THE CREATIVE ABUNDANCE MODEL takes existing sheltered workshop spaces and programs and turns them into places where people of all abilities are encouraged to experiment and investigate through their own personal talents and assets. What they discover is then worked into the larger goal of job creation and community outreach. The Creative Abundance Model draws on resources that we already have in communities across the country: large spaces where people gather, also known as "sheltered workshops." These spaces, for the most part, already contain everything that we need to implement this new model. All it takes to do so is a shifting of the furniture and the mind. Such a shift turns these spaces into incubators of discovery, where creativity can flourish and previously separated communities can come together.

The Creative Abundance Model also offers a compromise. There is a national movement to close sheltered workshops and move people into integrated community settings. Many family members and service providers, though, are saying, "Wait! That won't work for everybody." It is not our intent to resolve this debate. It is also not our intent to see every sheltered workshop closed. What we offer is an option for using what we already have and transforming it to provide opportunities for integration, collaboration, and greater community acceptance for individuals who have perceived intellectual disabilities. We want to revolutionize programming, but that doesn't mean that we need to start all over again. We propose using existing spaces and resources, revolutionizing the programming. As with every movement or revolution or evolution, there must be conciliation. The Creative Abundance Model offers one path toward a creative and productive middle ground.

A unique and compelling characteristic of many people with developmental disabilities is their inherent creativity. An average person with a developmental disability is much more likely to jump into a creative endeavor than is an average member of the larger community. They worry less about whether they are doing it right, whether they look silly, or whether they have the ability to embrace the process. They can enjoy painting simply because it feels good to paint, to see the colors mix and images form. They get lost in this moment. "Typical people" often have voices in their head that they have to squash before even attempting to put brush to paper: "What do you think you are doing? What a waste of time. You have no talent. People are going to judge you." And guess what? They talk themselves out of creating. But if you put materials out on a table in front of a group of people with cognitive differences and invite them to investigate, you will have participation and enthusiasm from some of the finest, most creative people on the planet.

Through creative investigation, we discover individual interests and talents while delivering programming options within a group. If we say, "Replicate this thing" (as with crafts), we are just asking people to re-create someone else's idea. If their gingerbread figures do not look like the original example, they have fallen short. We often see a staff member jump in and finish the project to make it look like everyone else's. There is little creativity involved in replicating something. It is already designed and created. It has nothing to do with the individual. Accepting and embracing the idea that a project doesn't have to be a perfect copy of something is the first step into individual exploration.

Instead, take that paint, pencil, and paper and begin to draw and investigate. *That* is something new. There is evidence of self, some-

Jenny's beautiful fireweed flower drawing was enlarged onto a piece of plywood using an overhead projector. The wood was painted black, and colorful hand-painted fabric (repurposed sheets) was cut out and laminated onto the wood, creating the surface design and mimicking Jenny's original drawing. (HOPE STUDIOS, ANCHORAGE, ALASKA)

thing to talk about, and something through which others can see the creative energy of the designer. Now we are talking. If a person draws a portrait of her best friend, it tells a story about her. The artist can give it as a gift. Her friend hangs it in her office, and perhaps someone else asks the artist to draw him or her. The artist starts a portrait business! Someone loves her work and wants her to draw his pet. She starts making paintings of dogs. The local Humane Society has a show of her work. As a special incentive, people who adopt dogs in December also receive a portrait of their new pet. Another person helps make a drawing into a silver charm, and a fundraiser is held for the local dog shelter. The local news channel runs a story about this project, and other cities want to replicate what was done and sell the charms. This is not crazy talk. This is how events unfold and opportunities open up. Nothing exists until we first imagine, start making, and respond to opportunity.

What if people are not interested in visual art? What if they are not interested in painting, drawing, or sculpting? What is important is what they *are* interested in! What if they are drawn to theater, dance, magic, singing, poetry, fashion, comedy, or gardening? The process is no different. In explaining the Creative Abundance Model, we will use art as the primary example, but the concepts can apply to any area of interest.

The Creative Abundance Model takes existing workshop spaces and turns them into places where people can feel free to take risks, be creative, and explore. It also turns sheltered workshops into community centers, where everyone can feel supported, welcomed, and encouraged to be a creative being.

We have never come across a group of people more forgiving and patient than this population, who are just waiting for their support systems to get it together and provide the environment for investigation and creative exploration. It is as if they had been waiting all their lives for these opportunities. If we only had a magic wand, people with disabilities could be creative, outgoing, inventive, individualistic beings. Oh, wait! They already are!

THE EVOLUTION

THE TERM *sheltered workshop* is used to refer to a wide range of segregated vocational and nonvocational programs for individuals with disabilities, such as sheltered employment, adult activity centers, work activity centers, and day treatment centers. Sheltered workshops or work centers historically have provided rehabilitation services, training, and/or employment opportunities to individuals with disabilities. The term has been used generally to describe facilities that employ people with disabilities exclusively or primarily. Sheltered employment programs are designed to assist individuals who, for whatever reason, are viewed as not capable of working in a competitive employment setting in their local community. These programs differ extensively in terms of their mission, services provided, and funding sources. Currently, most sheltered employment services are operated through private, not-for-profit organizations funded through a variety of state, federal, and local funding sources. Many work centers no longer refer to themselves as "sheltered workshops," nor do they perceive themselves as offering sheltered employment. Whatever the changes in terminology, however, the design and function of these programs have remained the same.

For more than forty years, sheltered workshops have been perceived as the answer to the past horrors of institutionalization. In reality, sheltered workshops are simply smaller institutions within community settings. Their similarity to institutions is far greater than their difference. They are similar in design and location. Like institutions, sheltered workshops are segregated and often located on the outskirts of town. They are similar in program delivery. Like institutions, sheltered workshops expect conformity, compliance, and adherence to a routine. Value is placed on being the same, rather than being different or outside of the "norm." Individuals are expected to complete mundane, routine tasks that have little value other than a meager paycheck that is based on what they can produce when compared to a "normal worker" standard.

Sheltered workshops are designed to be exactly the opposite of what their missions say they are. Their mission statements extoll lofty ideals and values. They talk about individuality, community inclusion, collaboration, and meaningful lives. In reality, they are places of conformity, exclusion, isolation, and meaningless activity. Most important, do agencies believe in their mission and vision statements? These declarations are positive. They make the promise of providing the place for individuals and families to dream and live rich lives: connecting, living, and working in community. For the typical agency, these statements are dreams that they *want* to come true. Deep down, however, they don't believe the dreams *can* come true.

Mission statements are also used to sell the program to incoming prospects. Once these folks with Medicaid dollars begin receiving services in a sheltered workshop, they are typically there for life, with little expectation for growth or advancement of their potential or graduation from original services. And the program has no incentive for enabling people to leave. If they go, the money goes too. Until funding is based on outcomes rather than delivery of services, organizations will have little motivation to change.

Staff members are hired to maintain a norm, not to encourage creativity. This tendency leads to a cadre of staff members who are attracted to work that has an expected outcome and a systematic approach to arriving at a predetermined outcome. The approach to recruiting, hiring, training, and retaining staff members has the same unintended (or intended, depending on the organization) result of maintaining the status quo. Quantifiable markers determine success: attendance, meeting quotas for number of pieces assembled, following behavior plans, keeping people in their seats. In other words, employees have been hired to keep the factory going. However, the workshop is *not* a factory. These programs are places where people, who happen to have perceived differences, come for services and/or work because a promise was made to them. The agency's mission stated that the workshop would support them in discovering their best selves. They were going to have a lifetime of investigation and self-discovery, to be respected as individuals and receive person-centered programming. It all sounded so good.

Investigation and experimentation usually live only in those mission statements. Risk is not rewarded. Inside the workshop, a culture of bullies maintains the status quo. It is important not to shake up the system because, when all is said and done, the most important thing to the staff and administration is keeping the jobs they know and are comfortable in. Agencies protect the bureaucracy to the detriment of quality programming. Staff members worry, "If we introduce new programming, and it is successful, will there be a place for me? If these people are not dependent on my caring for them, what will I do?" Such fears have no place in exploring innovative approaches.

To do something new is to be vulnerable. To take risks and to explore new possibilities expose a person to both criticism and success. We need to develop a culture in which risk is rewarded and advances are celebrated. Let's make the group stronger and the organization lively with growth. One good idea or experience encourages the next. There is a Japanese proverb that says, "The nail that sticks out gets hammered down." Let's not hammer down what stands out; let's hang our hat and dreams on that nail!

Maybe such opportunities are not offered because staff and administrators feel that it is unreasonable to expect people who have developmental disabilities to become deeply engaged. The fear is that they are not capable of anything more than capping a pen or stuffing an envelope. Is it cruel to set the bar higher because they might fail and be embarrassed and defeated? Absolutely *not!*

It is time to begin looking at sheltered workshops differently. It is time for the next step in their evolution. It is time for a revolutionary new way of offering services to people. The Creative Abundance Model is not a theoretical approach. It is a real way to develop innovative and creative programming that is interesting, engaging, and meaningful to people, their families, the staff, and the community.

THE REVOLUTION

WHY HAVE WE held on to the sheltered workshop model for so long? People are different and community opportunities are varied, yet we continue to replicate factory-like institutional settings in which people are expected to conform to the demands of the assembly line. If they are not working, their free time is spent doing jigsaw puzzles, filling coloring books, stringing plastic beads, or doing word-finding games. These activities are typically self-directed and relieve the staff from the responsibility of providing activities. The people who show up at the workshop and who are not engaged with work or with an interesting activity take to these default options for self-preservation. If they do not become involved with something—anything—they retreat into themselves: they become lethargic, they sleep, and ultimately they fail to thrive. Engagement is connection. Without purpose and without connection, we, as social beings, begin to wither, and the opposite is also true. To avoid boredom people will create their own stimulation, positive or negative.

Programming in such places has changed little, if at all, since the 1970s. It is not because the services are so great. It is not because we have found *the* solution in providing programming. In reality, it is everything we do *not* want in programming: segregated environments, exclusion from the larger community, and limited work opportunities, most of which are mind numbing. Assembly-line work is repetitive and a poor fit for people with physical challenges. It is difficult to explain why we have held on to this paradigm for so many years and why we have decided to replicate such a dysfunctional service model across the United States.

In the 1980s, many organizations started community employment programs. There is no doubt that employment in a traditional job is a viable outcome for many people with disabilities. People with developmental disabilities across the country have successfully obtained jobs, and examples of creative and interesting employment outcomes are abundant. Almost daily you can find a story on Facebook, Twitter, Tumblr, or LinkedIn about an individual with a disability who has opened a restaurant, received an award at work, or run a marathon with a coworker. But the number of people who have successfully obtained jobs through the traditional pathway of supported employment is woefully inadequate.

Efforts to increase employment outcomes seldom amount to more than catchy new titles, political posturing, and rule changes. What has not changed is the method used to find jobs for people. What has not changed is our way of thinking. Instead of looking at how we can maintain traditional workshop-based employment for people with disabilities, we should be finding new ways for individuals to earn income. Engagement in income-producing ventures is a flexible approach that allows the talent, creativity, and skills of the person to be at the forefront. Like anyone else, people with disabilities who earn income by doing something that they are passionate about have a higher likelihood of success. If a person can earn income by playing the organ at local church services, painting portraits of dogs, or housesitting for neighbors' cats, who are we to say that these are not viable jobs? Continuing to define "employment" as a job in the community, for at least twenty hours per week, in which a person earns a wage at or above the federal minimum will lead us down the same old path of low employment outcomes. If we judged everyone by this standard, many consultants, artists, musicians, photographers, public speakers, nannies, and housekeepers would be considered underemployed or unemployable.

Forty years ago, we could not imagine walking around with a handheld device that gave us access to phone service, the Internet,

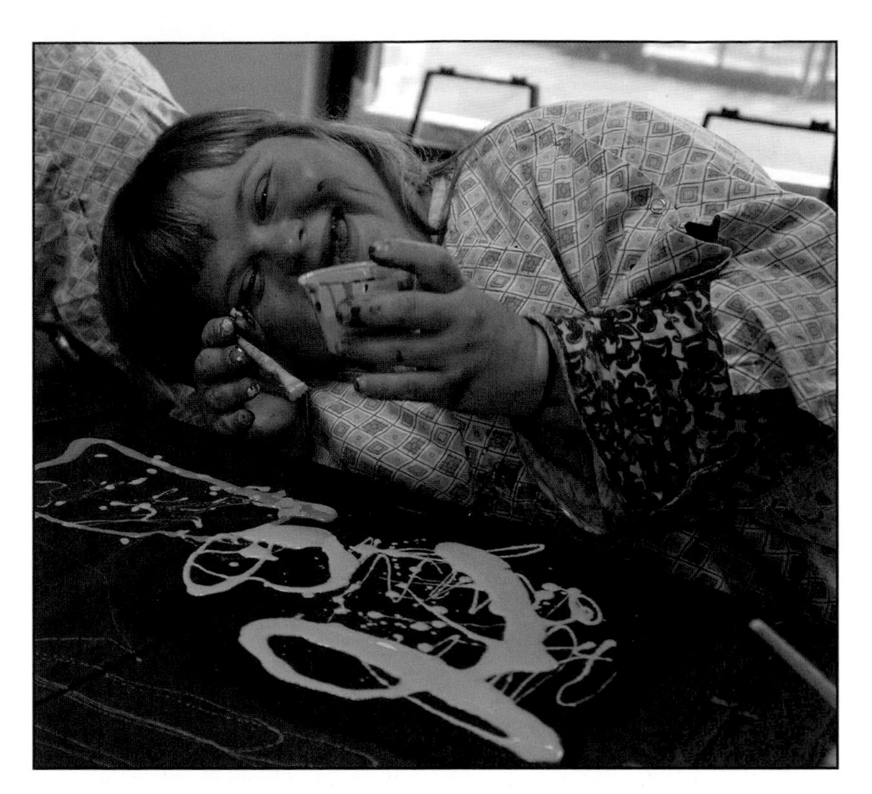

Courtney exploring her style. (UP AND BEYOND ART STUDIO, HILLSBORO, OHIO)

social media sites, movies, and interactive games. Most of us were still trying to figure out how to use an electric typewriter. When we think about how many things have evolved in our society during that time, we are amazed by the advances in technology, civil rights, medicine, and global networking. Despite all these changes, however, little has been done to enhance the day-to-day lives of people who attend segregated day programs or sheltered workshops. When we look at the sheer number of people who remain in these environments, it is clear that there is a lot to do.

Imagine sheltered workshops as places where communities come together to explore, discover, and create. We already have everything we need: space, people, and materials. It is time to rethink the possibilities and combine these assets to design a plan for a better life. The better the program, the better the lives of people, including staff, families, and community. It is time to shift our thinking from a manufacturing economy to a creative economy.

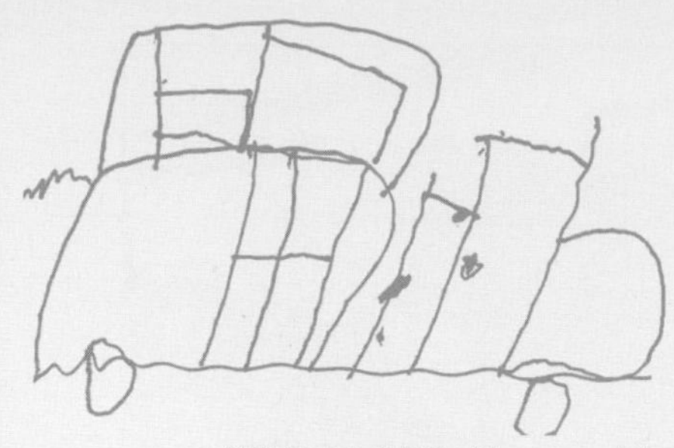

WHEN I BEGAN to read through the first few chapters of this book, I must admit that I was terribly saddened by the kind of place my beloved workshop has become. Not only are we failing miserably to follow the mission statement, but we're hiding behind it in the way we serve our individuals. These chapters were very hard to swallow, but ultimately, they pushed me to read on. I needed to know that it was all going to be okay and that the answers I was now looking for were coming to me in the following pages. I needed validation that I hadn't purposefully stunted the imaginations and sometimes even the rights of the individuals I truly love.

As the studio coordinator, I'm constantly accused of "not doing anything" and "having the easiest job in the building." Ironically, in the past six months that I have worked with the artists in the studio, I have worked harder than I've ever worked in the workshop. It is just a different kind of work now. I am no longer straining to control situations and behaviors. I now am trying to feed and inspire people. Sitting down with the team to figure out why the individual is doing this or that is no longer a priority to me. It doesn't matter why, it just matters that it is a part of this person. It's part of who they are. Now it's up to me to figure out how to embrace this characteristic and help it grow into something beautiful. I have one individual who will paint only with the color blue. She loves it! Unfortunately, the market for solid blue, 2' × 2' canvases is at an all-time low right now. I sat in the studio for two full hours one day, pondering the possibilities for this individual's obsession with "smurfizing" everything she touches. I look back at my actions, and I know that my coworkers had to be cussing me in their minds as I sat with my eyes glazed over while they worked their butts off trying to keep everyone else involved with activities. In my mind, I was in a zone that would ultimately pay off for this individual. In their minds, I was the lazy golden child, sitting in the corner doing nothing . . . again.

When Susan Dlouhy (coauthor of this book) came into Highland County, it was to help us prepare for our CARF and state accreditation surveys. She did this by bringing in program consultants and artists in residence Patty Mitchell (coauthor of this book) and Robert Lockheed, shuffling the staff around, and taking away some highly protected desks. They all thought, What a bitch! Although I pride myself on trying always to put the needs of the individuals first, these changes were hard—for some staff, even traumatizing. I truly believe that if on day one of Susan's reign the staff had been required to read UPCYCLING SHELTERED WORKSHOPS the necessary changes would have been accepted as just that: necessary! It's hard to teach an old dog new tricks, but after reading this book, I now realize that it is possible to change ideas and actions. After so many years of being conditioned (as a staff person in this field) to assist, assist, assist, I know that it is going to take time to retrain myself instead, to enable, inspire, and then get out of the way. I am so excited after reading the book. I feel rejuvenated out of the mundane, into this new world of opportunities not only for the individuals I serve but also for myself.

So thank you for this book, or, as I like to call it, "the kick in the butt I needed." Individuals no longer will be forced to work in a black-and-white newspaper workshop but now will have the opportunity to explore the crayon box of inspiration, imagination, and expression that is the Up and Beyond Art Studio. I now know that we aren't just a part of the revolution. We are the revolution! And anything is possible!

JORDAN FREEZE, STUDIO MANAGER,
UP AND BEYOND ART STUDIO, HILLSBORO, OHIO

4 THE CREATIVE ABUNDANCE MODEL FRAMEWORK

THE CREATIVE ABUNDANCE MODEL can best be described as a context that surrounds the way services are provided. The Creative Abundance Model is based on the interconnectedness of community and the wealth of creative spirit that already exists. The more you trust the creative process, the more opportunities will find you. Under the current system, staff members have a powerful and direct influence on how programming is offered; this framework is built around the established roles and responsibilities of each position.

Board members are charged with establishing the overall mission of the organization. If the mission is to offer innovative, responsive, and creative programming, then it is incumbent upon the board to hire and support an administrator who can fulfill that mission. The board must continuously evaluate the administrator in terms of his or her ability to achieve the mission.

Administrators are responsible for ensuring that resources and structures are in place to support and encourage innovative, responsive, and creative programming opportunities. These resources include funding, adequate staff in terms of quantity and quality, environment, and organizational policies that support the mission. The administration must set a clear vision for the organization, one that values and encourages the desired outcomes. Nothing should get in the way of the mission.

Managers provide the day-to-day structure that enables staff to move forward and be their best selves and to encourage innovative, responsive, and creative programming opportunities. This structure includes operating procedures, clear expectations for how staff members interact with people, quality benchmarks, and evaluation of qualitative outcomes. Managers must be willing to make tough decisions when staff members are not able to execute the model. These decisions affect people's lives. There is no room for staff members who will not, for whatever reason, carry out the mission. Managers and others who like black-and-white outcomes will struggle at first with the Creative Abundance Model. Flexibility is what makes it work.

Staff members in turn must support the platform for participants to move forward and be their best selves and encourage participation in those innovative, responsive, and creative programming opportunities. Staff members who have a broad range of interests outside of work are often the most successful in this model. When they can share a talent or interest, they have a stronger commitment to the outcome. Staff members need to let go of the notion of being a supervisor or instructor and embrace the role of collaborator. Letting go of control and power is essential. The outcome is not about a finished product or a predetermined result; it is the process or investigation.

The second major component of the Creative Abundance Model is a shift away from a manufacturing economy and toward a creative economy. Outside the sheltered workshop environment, we are making this same shift. John Howkins published *The Creative Economy* in 2001 and completely revised it in 2013. Howkins writes, "The creative economy is based on a new way of thinking and doing. The primary inputs are our individual talent or skill. These inputs may be familiar or novel; what is more important is that our creativity transforms them in novel ways. In some sectors, the output value depends on the uniqueness; in others, on how easily it can be copied and sold to large numbers of people. The heartlands are art, culture, design and innovation." This is where workshops can have an edge in designing and creating their own employment options and partnering with the larger community. We can begin identifying workshop programs as art and business incubators or as creative industries. The Creative Abundance Model does not define work as the enemy. The model affords people opportunities to earn income, develop new purpose, generate connections with the larger community, and become less dependent on government supports.

STAGES

The Creative Abundance Model has twelve stages. We believe that every organization will go through each stage at some point in its implementation of the model. The order and speed with which any given organization progresses through these stages are unique. Some organizations are very methodical in their approach to change: examining each step, developing accompanying procedures, realigning their mission, and making sure funding is secured. Other organizations are risk takers. They jump on new ideas, making necessary adjustments along the way. A certain amount of risk is inherent in any major change. Understanding some of the events that may occur along the way will make this exciting journey a little less daunting.

GRANTING PERMISSION

Granting permission is one way of describing the process of letting go, something that must occur at all levels of an organization. The administration must be encouraging and enthusiastic about support staff's experiments with new approaches and projects. Support staff must be encouraging and enthusiastic about each individual's exploration of new possibilities. Historically, as organizations evolved

THE CREATIVE ABUNDANCE MODEL

1 GRANTING PERMISSION
It's OK to let go of tight control and invite investigation

2 FUNDING
Engaging programming encourages higher attendance and community integration

3 STAFF ACCEPTANCE AND IMPLEMENTATION
Create an exciting workplace where staff share interests and passions too

4 YOUR WAITRESS DOESN'T EAT YOUR FOOD
Prepare the space, materials, and positive atmosphere with the goal of individual exploration

5 POWER TO THE PEOPLE
Flexible programming responds to each individual's interests and rhythm

6 COMMUNITY PARTNERSHIPS
Become a jewel of the community

7 CULTURE SHIFT
Celebrate community and individual interests by developing new programming through what you already have

8 EXPECTATIONS SHIFT
We can always do better and have even more FUN!

9 ENVIRONMENT
Design spaces to encourage different exploration: theater, art, music, sport, etc.

10 CONTINUOUS EVOLUTION OF DISCOVERY
The process of exploration becomes your programming

11 THE NATURE OF ATTRACTION
Generate FUN, beauty, joyous spectacle...and the people/community will come

12 SHARE THE ABUNDANCE
Be open, respond to opportunity, and share

Info Graphic by Colleen Flayler. Artwork: Collaboration with Carolyn and visiting artists Wendy Minor-Viny and Patty Mitchell. (COMMUNITY CONNECTIONS, ATHENS, OHIO)

Rita, Susan Dlouhy (author), and Aaron in a drumming circle. To the rhythm of the beat, participants shared their likes, dreams, and humor.
(HOPEWELL INDUSTRIES, COSHOCTON, OHIO)

within the traditional sheltered workshop model, a highly regimented, controlled environment was necessary. After all, who really wants to sit all day, being told exactly what to do and how to do it, within a system that dictates every choice and determines whether you are "good" or "bad" by a preconceived standard?

We often hear staff members refer to "my group," "my guys," or "my individuals." This false sense of ownership is something that needs to change. People who feel controlled do not feel free to take risks, explore, and be creative. They live in fear of making a mistake rather than with the joy of creating something new. Staff members whose supervisors encourage them to take risks will, in turn, pass this mentality along to the people they support. Granting permission is all about creating the environment to take risks. It all starts at the top. Pass it along!

For the Creative Abundance Model to work, administrators and staff members must give themselves permission to release control, as well as give up heavily regimented environments and expectations. Administrators often fall into the trap of ritualized scheduling to hold staff accountable. The belief has been that if there is no ritualized schedule, there is no way to tell whether employees are doing their jobs, and there will be chaos among the individuals. To begin

Artist in residence Robert Lockheed and artist Kim celebrating beauty.
(ART ROCKS STUDIO, CARROLL, OHIO)

making the shift, administrators and staff must create the space, issue an invitation to explore, and provide encouragement.

The structure should encourage curiosity. The interests of the people then become the heart and direction of programming. Structure is not a negative thing. We need structure. It becomes negative, however, when the structure becomes the program and dominates the individuals, squashing and discouraging investigation.

Think about our highway system. Highways are built to provide us with the opportunity to travel from one place to another, but we have the choice of where to go. We can go to Florida or Minnesota. So it is with the Creative Abundance Model: it provides the structure, but the choice of where to go is an individual one.

Or think about a playground. The playground equipment (or structure) is provided, but the children use their imaginations to play. There is no "right" way to climb on a jungle gym. How many times have you seen a child climb up a slide rather than slide down? The structure is there, but the exploration is individual. In a similar way, the Creative Abundance Model requires letting go of what happens within the structure.

IF WE GOOGLE the word "boundary," the definition is "a line that marks the limits of an area; a dividing line." We all have boundaries in everyday life. We follow laws, policies, and procedures at work; social etiquette creates other boundaries in how we interact with others. For the most part, these boundaries are positive, helping create structure and a sense of comfort. We know how fast we are expected to drive on our way to work. We know that we are expected to be at work at a certain time, to stay for so many hours, and to complete certain tasks while we are there. We know that we behave differently with our coworkers than we do with our family because the boundaries are different. Is predictability always good? What if the rules or boundaries begin to feel like a limitation?

When we are trying to expand our knowledge, try new things, and meet new people, boundaries have to move with us. For people who do not have a disability, this is usually a pretty simple process; you decide that you are interested in something, decide whether you are willing to take a risk, and if the answer is yes, you do it! Whatever the risk is, the chance for a new experience makes it worth it. For someone who has a disability, this may not be so easy. As paid support or advisors, we are charged with the task of helping people learn boundaries in all aspects of their lives and to create structure to keep them safe. Living life fully and stretching those boundaries is not always safe or comfortable. As advocates or supports in the current model of sheltered settings, employees are conflicted. We are charged with creating safety while pushing boundaries to try new things. The predictable structure of the day programs of the past is no longer. Is your head spinning yet? How do we create new opportunities and experiences that have an element of risk, like volunteering in community settings, participating in art exhibits open to all artists, or seeking community employment and social networks not comprised of people paid to be there? The answer will be different for every person. It should be based on how he or she wants to redefine the boundaries. If failure is never an option, neither is success. Push the boundaries and see where life goes. Let the person's interests guide the process. Everyone should have the opportunity to build a life based on experiences, good and bad. Decision making gets easier with practice!

ANDRIA KLEINER, ADULT DEVELOPMENTAL SERVICES MANAGER,
RIVERSIDE OF MIAMI COUNTY, TROY, OHIO

I MET PROGRAM consultants/artists in residence Patty Mitchell and Robert Lockheed when our organization, a center serving adults with disabilities, was going through a very tough time. We had recently lost our largest client, and dealing with that change convinced us that simply finding a new client wasn't the answer. Although it was a scary time, we decided that the future required a new vision, one focused on providing a wealth of opportunities so the people we serve could find those things that make them happy and, hopefully, a way for them to bring value into their community.

Our employees were wonderful and ready for the challenge, but they needed help in the way of inspiration. Patty and Robert had been referred to us prior to our change, and the timing couldn't have been better. Vickie was one of our veteran employees, and she was inspired to create a new art program. Together we met with Patty and Robert to plan our event. I was concerned that Patty and Robert's efforts would focus too much on art and not enough on creating joy in the process of change. I couldn't have been more wrong.

Patty and Robert embraced the concept beautifully (or maybe I embraced theirs—it's hard to tell), and what they created over their two-week residency was nothing less than stellar. Out of the 140 people served in our facility, 120 of them enjoyed the program that Patty, Robert, Vickie, and a host of other employees and volunteers brought to life. All the things you would expect were there: incredible creativity, wonderful art projects, and a whole lot of smiles. There is an aspect of Patty and Robert's work that never ceases to amaze me. They can take the creative vision of an artist and display it in a way that enhances the art without losing the original artist's vision.

The work we do is often very rule oriented. We establish a rigid set of rules, even referring to it with pride as a consistent environment. Here is the secret of Patty and Robert's success: they wallow in the chaos. By exploring a virtually unlimited set of opportunities, many of the people who participate in the program find something that brings them joy. A few even discover their passion. Every time that happens, the rules naturally fall away, and people come to the program for the simple joy of being there and sharing their talent. I can't imagine anything better than that.

Of course, the real question is whether an experience like this can be sustained. Our initial efforts at change resulted in twenty-three new discovery groups, ranging from creating art to helping at the local Humane Society. After a year and a half, some of those groups didn't last, and some changed. A number of those groups, however, continued and flourished. The Green Machine partnered with local master gardeners to create a 6,800-square-foot vegetable garden that brings some needed pay to its workers, and the excess food goes to the local homeless shelter. Other groups volunteer in the community, build furniture, and cook. And the art program? They became Art Rocks Studio—a collaborative art program that still serves a huge number of people each month. All of these programs owe their start to the passion of our staff and to the lesson in creativity and joy that Patty and Robert shared so generously with us.

RAY SCHMIDT, DIRECTOR OF QUALITY, INNOVATION, AND PLANNING, FAIRFIELD COUNTY BOARD OF DEVELOPMENTAL DISABILITIES, LANCASTER, OHIO

We need to look at more than just the outcomes of service. The process is just as important. Remember, artists don't start with a finished piece of art. There are layers and layers of ideas and investigation of materials that, when combined, develop into something new. Set big-picture goals for employees that stress flexibility and ingenuity and then support those employees in developing their path, investigating ways to support individuals working through their process, and meeting their goals.

The administration envisions a new way and then grants staff permission to be their best selves. We need to change our measure of value in a staff member. Currently, we focus our orientation and training programs on things like health and safety, reporting unusual incidents, universal precautions, and documentation skills. We spend little, if any, time on customer service, encouraging creativity, and developing innovative and creative team members. A good staff member is defined as someone who has good attendance, completes accurate and timely documentation, and has minimal disturbances from his or her group. These qualities are not enough to define success on the job. We can and must create more interesting and expansive employment opportunities for staff.

Continuing to evaluate people on the basis of their attendance, documentation skills, and ability to keep their group quiet will perpetuate the current service delivery system. Evaluating staff on the basis of their ingenuity and ability to achieve amazing outcomes will raise programming to a new level that is beyond our current scope of thinking. The administration does not create the programming; it encourages the combining of what already exists into something new and fabulous.

A friend of Patty's, musician J. D. Hutchison, once said, "Mitchell, you are not inventing the egg; you are making the omelet." As a young visiting artist, Patty used to get full of anxiety before doing a collaborative art project in a sheltered workshop. When she heard this remark, the way ahead became clear.

It is not up to us to design what exactly is going to happen—we should have no preconceived notion of the intended results or the craft model. That would not be an authentic exploration. The job is to create the environment and provide the materials for the explora-

Artists in residence Robert Lockheed and Patty Mitchell (author) facilitated a two-week collaborative art residency with the intention of building a bench. Driftwood was collected, painted, and made into a highly decorative bench and sculpture. (HOPE COMMUNITY RESOURCES, KODIAK, ALASKA)

tion. As the project progresses, the artist can use his or her skills and experience to combine an individual's work into a collaborative installation (such as a mural, sculpture, or quilt). Success does not lie solely in delivering the final art piece. With experience and confidence, you can structure the studio to celebrate the surrender of the art process to the artists. It is exciting to see what happens. You will be constantly surprised and thrilled by people's work. How can you possibly anticipate what people will do or be interested in? As your

confidence grows, you can let go of more and more of the control. This is a mini version and a physical example of the approach the larger organization can take. You are not responsible for the details of the outcome or the design of new programming; just create the structure for authentic exploration with the anticipation of discovery. The process of exploration becomes your programming, and outcomes such as employment options, business opportunities, and art shows are the fruit.

Key Points

- Physical and programmatic structures are simply vehicles for exploration.
- Surrender the process
- Encourage people to follow their own creative paths
- If a project starts out as an herb garden and evolves into a butterfly sanctuary, it's okay!

FUNDING

In the traditional sheltered workshop model, funding follows the people receiving services. By showing up at the day program, they have attracted dollars to the program. Regardless of the source of funding (for example, Medicaid, local tax dollars, and state subsidies), the income for the program is generated by attendance. Sure, there is an expectation that the organizations follow some rules, complete some documentation, and adhere to some definition of quality. But the bottom line is that people attending the program generate dollars.

There is nothing in these funding models that prevents organizations from offering high-quality services as opposed to mediocre ones. Many programs spend more time figuring out how to manipulate funding to maintain what they already have than using the funding to improve their programming. State provider associations rally together any time there is a change in funding, in order to protect the status quo. Rarely are these funding changes seen as an opportunity to try something different.

Medicaid funding is not the wolf disguised in sheep's clothing that it is sometimes made out to be. It is actually the fairy godmother. Medicaid waivers encourage creativity and innovation. States get to submit their ideas for new service models. Waivers are exactly what they say they are: permission to waive some federal requirements and still remain eligible to receive Medicaid dollars. Waivers are vehicles that states can use to test new ways to deliver and pay for services.

Surely this Creative Abundance Model is too radical to be supported by traditional funding, especially Medicaid—right? In reality, the funding can be used in concert with the Creative Abundance Model. There is no trick to Medicaid funding. In many states, Medicaid is actually pushing organizations to be more innovative. There are several types of waivers designed around the concepts of self-determination and self-directed activities that provide opportunities for individuals to design, direct, and pay for their own services. These waivers work well with the Creative Abundance Model because they allow flexibility.

Nor are other traditional funding sources necessarily a barrier to utilizing the Creative Abundance Model. In fact, attendance-based funding is the perfect vehicle to bring about change. Payment is received when people attend programming. When people are authentically engaged through programming options, they are more likely to attend regularly. Many workshops see a drastic drop in attendance when there is no work available. Is assembly work so stimulating that people can't bear to come in when there isn't any? Or is assembly work only slightly more interesting than coloring, watching movies, and playing Uno? Traditional programming also emphasizes the importance of the paycheck. No matter how meager the check, the reward (or carrot) is payday.

All that being said, significant changes are on the horizon. Funding changes often can be the impetus for service delivery changes. It is imperative to provide services that bring in the dollars needed to continue the program. Medicaid waivers were intended to support people in integrated community settings. Most day service programs, however, have supported people in segregated, sheltered settings. When funding no longer supports segregated services, change will follow. Organizations that are ready to embrace the change will survive. Organizations that bury their heads in the sand will not.

The Creative Abundance Model will position organizations to take advantage of these funding changes. It embraces change, risk taking, and flexibility. It is rooted in the concepts of integration, inclusion, and community. Transform your day program into an integrated, inclusive, diverse community center. Create an environment that the new funding models will support.

Key Points

- Funding can be aligned with the Creative Abundance Model.
- Demands for changes in the way services are delivered will make the Creative Abundance Model not only good business but a necessity.

STAFF ACCEPTANCE AND IMPLEMENTATION

Embracing change can be difficult. The unknown is scary. We tend to hang on to the familiar (even if we are miserable) instead of venturing into unchartered territory. Nowhere is it more difficult to make changes than in a sheltered workshop. The primary barrier to change is not the people who attend the program, however: it is the people who were hired to support them, the staff.

Many behaviors of staff members can be linked to institutional behaviors, to institutional thought; individuals must move at the same rate as the whole. But members of the group do not necessarily have the same individual interests, talents, or opportunities. No one thing will move each individual forward, but each individual success will move the collective forward. Individualized attention and person-centered responsive programming is diametrically opposed to institutionalized thinking.

Among staff members, protection of territory prevails: people, areas of the building, supplies, and equipment. You often hear com-

Papier-mâché goblin mask in process.

ments like "Nobody knows 'my people' as well as I do," "He won't work out well in another group," or "I'm the only one who can work with her." There are locked cabinets accessible only to certain staff members or protected space within the building that cannot be used by anyone else. When we begin to change the use of physical spaces by introducing new programming approaches, there is a natural tendency to "protect what is mine." After all, staff often have expended a significant amount of effort to create separation between themselves and the "clients." Those desks, tables, or work spaces have great meaning to them. Movement creates more anxiety for the staff than it does for the people receiving services, because staff members see it as a loss of power and control as well as a loss of territory. How am I going to get my paperwork done if I am sitting at a table with the "clients"? Where am I going to put my files? Where am I going to eat my lunch? Staff members may initially see change as a punishment. The people see it as something fun, exciting, and new. Even people who have difficulty with change in their routine or in their environment rarely take more than a couple of days to

adjust. Anticipating these types of reactions from staff members and addressing them with compassion is a necessary element of the change process.

Fear of change can increase the urge to maintain the current system or method of programming. Just because the staff is uncomfortable with the unknown is no excuse to not expect growth and discovery in programming. We are not social service agencies to support work programs for underqualified, stubborn, controlling staff members. Yet it is not appropriate to expect staff members who were hired to maintain institutionalized factory-style work training centers to develop and execute innovative programming on their own, without the support of the larger organization.

The traditional role of staff within workshops has been to replicate a predetermined set of standards. Work comes first, and no one should deviate from this norm. The Creative Abundance Model turns this culture upside down and inside out, declaring a revolution of opportunity. The staff must be on board and excited about their role in this evolution.

Staff members must learn to embrace the new way of thinking. Fear is not a motivator for change. Fear freezes people into holding on to what is familiar and taking no risk. When people fear for their livelihood, they become defensive and feel cornered. Under these conditions, the free flow of ideas will not happen. We also need to remember that many of these staff people may not have identifiable skills that would allow them to find work and equivalent pay on the outside. They perceive their situation as desperate and will defend what they have at any cost.

The situation, however, is not as hopeless as these staff members may perceive it to be. When the administration announces a move away from the sheltered workshop model, it must at the same time set a new tone and explain the new expectations so that staff members believe in the plan. When expectations and approach are demystified, buy-in begins as the staff comes to understand how the shift will benefit them. Everyone is interested in self-preservation, in not looking the fool, and in having purpose. Given opportunity, people begin to rise to new occasions.

It seems like everywhere we go, there is always at least one Betty Bully. Betty usually has been there at least ten years and somehow has earned an undeserved status by her seniority. She knows every reason why new ideas will not work. Every new idea has been tried in the past and failed. Betty is interested in personal control and power over others. She oversees her group with an iron fist. People are afraid of her and rarely complain about her actions. Her coworkers cringe in her presence and refuse to challenge her. She is not interested in implementing creative, innovative, responsive programming. She is interested in making sure that she has a job and that she is recognized and rewarded for her seniority.

Because we work in human services, we try to help Betty. We want Betty to be successful. Or, hoping that the situation will get better, we ignore Betty. She is only a few years from retirement; let's just ride it out. She has manipulated family members into thinking that the program cannot run without her. By doing nothing, however, we fail to protect the people whom we have been charged with the responsibility of serving. Sometimes you have to make the tough decision: Betty cannot continue in a position that is so influential in the lives of our most vulnerable and precious citizens.

Getting people into the right job is one of the most critical components of making a shift in programming. Staff often resist moving into different jobs. But people generally know what they can and cannot do. They know what situations work best for them. We need to ask them! Given the opportunity, they often will choose to move into the very position that was intended for them. Don't be afraid to move staff members around. Help them find out where and how they can best contribute to the organization.

By shifting the staff to positions that make the most of their abilities, we have a greater prospect for success. By accessing the likes and interests of the staff members, we can encourage them to share their talents with the individuals. They may have interests in activities like gardening, sewing, woodworking, bird-watching, hunting, walking, playing golf, dancing, singing, storytelling, reading, cooking, or community volunteering. Invite staff members to work through their personal interests and create programming through their passions and experiences.

Staff and administrators of many programs have written grants and built greenhouses only to find a few years later that they have become transparent sheds housing lawn mowers. Why didn't the

Rita exploring improvisation. (HOPEWELL INDUSTRIES, COSHOCTON, OHIO)

Samantha exploring improvisation. (HOPEWELL INDUSTRIES, COSHOCTON, OHIO)

greenhouses become lush places of growth and beauty? It is because the programs did not have staff interested in and dedicated to keeping the dream alive. Programs are not tools and equipment. Their power is in the spirit of the people who make up these agencies. State-of-the-art equipment will not operate itself. Without interested staff, a printing press for making etchings will sit there and become a storage table. But have a staff member curious about or experienced in making prints, and you will have a print department. As your program becomes known for making prints, you will attract future applicants with printmaking skills. Develop a gardening program, and you will attract like-minded applicants, volunteers, and individuals looking for programming. Continue programming that has no soul, and you will attract the same. You wouldn't ask a staff member who hates fishing to organize a fishing trip. Respect the person and follow the interest.

Part of staff development can become figuring out how to incorporate what staff members do in their free time or identifying what they have always wanted to explore and then adding those ideas into the programming. Examples of adaptable interests could include karate, horses, pets, bugs, travel, history, trivia, pranks, shadow puppets, or *The Price Is Right* . . . Now think of how each of these things could become a programming concept.

The Price Is Right exerts some kind of mind control over people. In most day programs we have visited, the hour when *The Price Is Right* airs is sacred time. We once encountered an organization that included *The Price Is Right* as part of its activity schedule. What makes this show so attractive to so many? Contestants running down the aisle and jumping up and down, excitement, lights, music, and prizes! What's not to like? What if you replicated *The Price Is Right* game show at your program? Lights flash, you call out names of people, they play games you create, win prizes, and the crowd goes wild! You can build a set out of cardboard—every step in making the set is an activity—and then perform in it. You don't have to have a massive thing built before you can stage the game show. You can start with a paper towel cardboard roll for a microphone, a pot lid and a stick for sound, and your own enthusiasm. The most important thing is enthusiasm! "But everyone will look at me and roll their eyes," you might say. Remember: it is your job to work through the fear and vulnerability to create something new. So what if you appear a little goofy? Be the Pied Piper! Build it and they will come! What better group of people to be vulnerable with? We are working with the world's most authentic, fun, and responsive people. They make our job easy! HAVE FUN!

Creative programming attracts creative people. Once the stage is set, the organization can begin to recruit staff members who have the skill sets to advance creative programming. If you have an art studio, you are more likely to attract an artist to join your staff. If you have a vibrant outdoor explorers club, you are more likely to attract someone who likes to hike, fish, and camp. It is not realistic to expect someone who loves the outdoors to be successful in your culinary program. If you are moving toward creative spaces, then new hires should be people who embrace the creative process.

Not every option will fit every organization, but the approach is the same: it must respond to the unique opportunities present within each organization. If you have NASCAR lovers, start building wooden cars and hold competitions for speed, distance, and aesthetic value. Write stories, investigate history, keep a scoreboard of active races on the wall, and build fantasy race teams. Design the programming through what connects you. NASCAR may not be a universal love, but maybe even nonfans will jump into making cars out of wood, painting, drawing the next design, sanding parts, attaching the wheels, taking prototypes to a local gallery to see whether they can be displayed, and connecting with a local vocational school and asking whether they would like to build cars, collaborate on a project, or have a picnic and car show. The point is that ideas grow and opportunities expand when you follow passion and energy. Within any project there is a place for people who want to participate. When it is understood that the design of a project grows in the direction of interest, expansion naturally follows the people's abilities. For example, let's say Cheryl only wants to paint circles. How can her interest be incorporated into the NASCAR theme? The answer: polka-dot cars.

In one studio, there was a woman who painted circles. For years she painted and painted, and her color combinations were amazing.

Artist Dan and Toni Lanzer, former studio manager. (SOARING ARTS STUDIO, NAPOLEON, OHIO)

Original drawing by Dan enlarged and made into a polka-dot car mural.

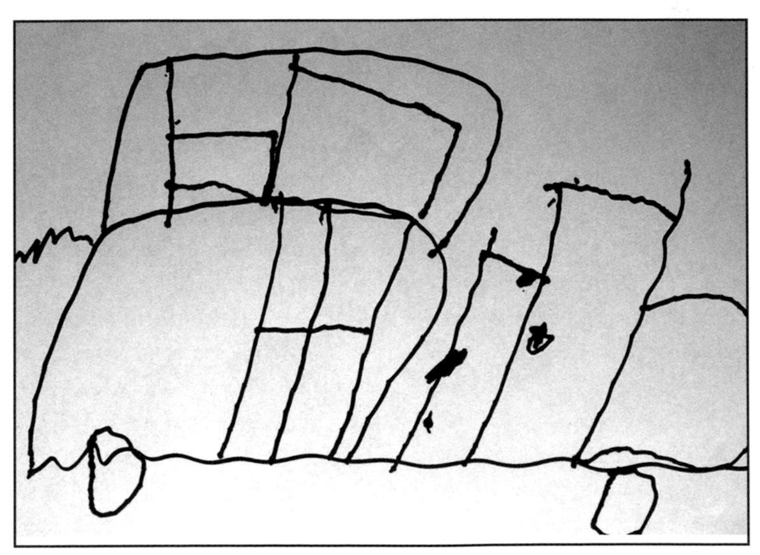

Professional artists would sit and watch her, trying to figure out her technique. She never took a break other than lunch and would stop only when the bus came. Each morning, she would shake with anticipation as her paint and brushes were prepared, and she worked with this level of enthusiasm for years. Her process was beautiful, and her work magnificent. When she moved to another county and into a different program, there was a crafts room, but her talent was not recognized. She had a job cleaning toilets and the opportunity to do crafts. Because the staff could not translate or even see her talent, she no longer had the opportunity to paint. Her talent lay dormant. The agency said, "This is an activity, this is not work. She needs to make money." It was not perceived that her art could be income producing. Because of that, she had limited opportunity to explore her genius.

When enjoyable activities are suggested as employment opportunities, there is often push back by staff. Do we have to suffer in order for an activity to be considered real work? Within a traditional program, there are clear lines. Over here is the activity area; over there is the work area. When these lines are blurred, it can create confusion for staff. For example, a common activity in sheltered workshops is threading plastic beads onto plastic string. The cheapest beads possible become the norm. What if those beads are switched out with beautiful glass beads? Same activity, different outcome.

The person who will sit for hours making necklaces for friends, visitors, and family members, while wearing four to six pieces around her neck, can thus become part of a jewelry-making business. Yes, there are problems to solve and questions to answer. We don't have those kinds of beads. Where can we get them? How do we pay for them? How long are the necklaces? How do they attach? Julie can only string, she can't tie knots. How much do we sell these for? How much is she going to make? Is it worth her time? (She has been sitting in the workshop stringing beads for ten years! If she makes twenty dollars, this is leaps and bounds beyond what was previously expected.) How do we market them? Can she keep up with orders? What is the name of her business? She can't make change.

All of these "problems" have answers. And as the opportunities grow, different answers will present themselves. There are multiple

Brendell and Kelly with the beautiful jewelry they made using felted wool, repurposed fabric, and shells. Thanks to staff member Brendell, an experienced jewelry designer, for sharing her skills.
(ACCESSPOINT RI, CRANSTON, RHODE ISLAND)

answers for every moment. There is never only one solution. You make the best decision you can in the moment. Art making is a succession of decisions. It is training for life. Let it unfold and celebrate the obstacles as opportunity: opportunity for outreach into the community, for partnerships, and for expansion. Think like an artist.

For an artist, obstacles are not negative. They are opportunities to intersect with other opportunities or situations waiting for solutions. Where there are no problems, there is no movement. Obstacles are expected. Solutions invite new vision. Not all answers present themselves at the beginning. Finding solutions is an unfolding and organic process. New opportunities will present themselves, but we need to train ourselves to not wait for the perfect moment when all the stars line up.

Staff members also must be aware of their own behavior and recognize how influential they can be. Let them ask the questions: Am I advancing programming? Am I getting in the way of someone's exploration? Am I imposing my judgment on this person and influencing them?

Making art demands focus. As artists become involved with their work, everything else falls away. The mind quiets, and the most important thing, in this moment, is this act of making. Being within this mind space is referred to as being in the flow. Staff members, even well-meaning ones, sometimes will come by and break the flow by saying, "Why is everyone so serious!" or by taking some paint on a brush and dotting someone's nose. This "joking" redirects attention and control back to the staff person. Our job is to create the structure for flow to happen and to share with staff how precious it is. When we find something in which people can lose themselves and be fully engaged, an exquisite goal has been met. There is also an incentive for staff members. Engaged, happy, productive people do not act out and seek stimulation through negative outlets. Ask staff members what happened before this type of programming was introduced, and they will say, "James would get up out of his seat twenty times a day and go to the restroom. We could never get him to sit still." Behavior plans didn't do it, and telling him to sit still didn't do it. Within the studio, the goal was not getting James to sit still. The

Lori painting for the first time. Out of a hat, tape, yarn, blue insulation board, and clamps, personalized adaptive equipment was made . . . and the results are fantastic! (WASCO, MARIETTA, OHIO)

goal was finding something that James loves to do. He loves to paint. He is happy and recognized for his talent, and the staff is not charged with constantly addressing his "behavior." This change relieves frustration for James and staff alike and creates more time and opportunity for staff to explore other possibilities for engagement. Everybody wins. The studio is not quiet and focused all the time; there are ample opportunities for laughing, talking, and joking. The atmosphere shifts like waves.

The staff's role shifts from setting up workstations, establishing quality control, and creating the illusion of work to facilitating, supporting, and problem solving. When individuals package a few nuts and bolts to collect a minuscule paycheck, the money is not the point. There is pride in getting a check on payday, holding it up, and showing everyone what they did. It is not about the actual check. It is pride in a job well done and in having done the best they can within a system that provides only the minimum of opportunity. We need to be better and do better to change the outcomes.

Key Points

- Positive expectations are a motivator for change.
- Getting people in the right jobs equals success.
- Be aware of how much influence you have.
- Start by building the programming around the talents and interests of the staff.

YOUR WAITRESS DOESN'T EAT YOUR FOOD

What part does the staff member play as a collaborator, if the programming is about the individuals exploring ideas and materials? The adventure is everyone's exploration. As facilitators, staff members can set the tone for the investigation, do a bit of construction, collect materials, and provide the structure for the investigation to happen.

What does "structure" mean? Think of everything that must be in place to experience a lovely dining experience in a restaurant. You have chosen a particular place based on a friend's recommendation. A friendly host welcomes you and leads you to your own space. The table is set and prepared for you: silverware, water, and napkin. You sit and are handed a menu. The menu creates options for you. If you did not have a menu and were asked, "What do you want?" it would be difficult to answer, because you would not know the available choices.

After going over the menu, you pick the salad and request the dressing on the side and extra tomatoes. The menu creates a structure, and the overall service of the restaurant responds to you, the customer. If the waitperson said, "We're not offering extra tomatoes today, and everyone gets Thousand Island dressing. It's already tossed in with the greens," you might not be happy. They are the same items, but not the way you want them. You see, it is easier for the cooks and servers to have one kind of salad dressing, mix up the salad in the morning so it is all organized, and prep it in serving bowls so that they have only to pull the bowls out of the refrigerator. To prepare a fresh salad for each guest would be a lot more work. The do-ahead

approach involves less effort and is less expensive and more convenient for the restaurant. But it is unsatisfying for the customer.

A restaurant you want to visit again and suggest to your friends would have service that is more responsive. The waitperson would offer choices of dressings and acknowledge your wishes: "You would like that with dressing on the side and with extra tomatoes? Can I get you anything else?" You were listened to, and the server met your request. Sometimes, of course, you cannot have exactly what you asked for: "I'm sorry, we're all out of tomatoes, but we can add extra mandarin oranges." This is not exactly what you were anticipating, but still you think, "Yes, that would be nice."

But what if you hear, "We're out of tomatoes, we're substituting oranges, and that is what you will be getting." When did Betty Bully become your waitress? It is the same offering but a different interaction. I am sure that you have had Betty Bully as a waitperson and that you also have had Positive Peggy. The waitperson sets the tone of your experience—the same food and physical space but a completely different experience.

Betty interrupts the conversation you are having with your friends to ask if you want anything. Peggy waits for your friend to finish the joke he is telling before intervening and asking if you are enjoying your meal and if you would like anything else.

Betty keeps interrupting, disrupting the flow of your dining experience, but then you cannot find her when you do need something. Your water glasses are empty, dirty plates clutter the table, and you really want a cup of coffee. There have been too many interruptions and then the frustration of not having what you need—and she also has a superior attitude, as if she does not have time to fill all those glasses. The food was not what you wanted, and the experience was not pleasant. You could not enjoy your conversation. The server did not make you feel respected and was dismissive of your needs.

Peggy, in contrast, filled your water glasses when they were half empty, taking care not to disturb the lively conversation at the table. She anticipated your need and took care of it. She cleared the table of dirty dishes but did not make you feel rushed. She brought the coffee pot to you and asked if you would like some. A cup was already

on the table, so you did not have to wait for her to go and come back; the area was prepared for more efficient and responsive service. Think like Positive Peggy: the customer's experience is in your response to his or her interests.

What if we offered the same level of service in our programs? "What do you want to do today?" is a big question and very difficult to answer if you do not know your choices. Develop a menu of options, even if it is a very limited one at first. You can start with large sheets of paper and some yellow, pink, and black paint with which people can draw or paint whatever they like. Imagine this conversation:

ARTIST: I would like a pencil to draw with first. I need a picture of a bunny.
STAFF MEMBER: Okay, I have a book you can look at.

ARTIST: I don't know what to do.
STAFF MEMBER: Would you draw a portrait of me?

ARTIST: Do you have a smaller brush?
STAFF MEMBER: Yes, here you go.

People start to settle in and experience that brush moving color across the paper. The colors combine. You see that swirls, bunnies, and portraits start to emerge. Seven people are around the table with the same materials but creating completely different things. Enjoy this moment.

As a collaborator or facilitator, think of your role as doing the things that other people cannot yet do. As soon as there is interest or an opportunity to shift responsibility to someone else, happily hand it off and expand the collaboration. If you are enlarging drawings onto plywood with an overhead projector and someone comes over and asks, "What are you doing?" explain while handing them the marker and inviting them to take over. "We're making wooden cutouts from drawings. Here is a marker; just trace this line you see that it is projecting onto the wood." What if Jamie really wanted to do that, but she is really shaky and the line would be all wobbly? Jamie

Jan demonstrating the joy of investigation: not being told what to do or how to do it but having the materials, space, and invitation to discover. It is that simple! (WASCO, MARIETTA, OHIO)

The waiter doesn't eat your food either! Robert and Nancy.

(WASCO, MARIETTA, OHIO)

wants to do it, and the line will have more movement, so it is fine. Evidence of Jamie's participation is now part of the project.

Now consider this scenario: You place your order at the restaurant, and the food comes out; it smells good and is exactly what you wanted. Then the waitress sits down and eats it for you! That is crazy! That would never happen! Think of yourself in the position of the waitress. Do not eat the food, and do not do the projects yourself because it is easier. It will end up looking the way you wanted it, and the activity will give you something to do. But if your involvement is at the expense of the artist's experience or participation, you should reconsider the options. You do not want your customer just sitting there watching you eat their dinner. This is a scenario that we often see when staff members are making crafts with people. There is such a desire to make that Popsicle-stick reindeer look exactly right that the staff member ends up completing the project.

Your role in the creative space is not as clearly defined as that of waitperson and customer. Facilitating projects and programming is a dance, and there is way more gray area. But if the little voice in your head says, "I am eating the food," it is time to release control.

Ask yourself, "Did I create a responsive, positive, individualized (dining) experience while supporting the needs of the group (customers)? What could have been better? What else could I introduce into the mix?" Try turning on music, opening up the curtains for better light, and setting the brushes on the table so that people do not have to ask for them. Get your water and paint prepared and on the table so people do not have to wait for service. We can always do better, change things up, and try this and that. Everything is always changing: participants, needs, skills, projects. You get to change and respond too. Every day is a new adventure in creating the best service possible and working with people to create new and interesting things. Keep it fresh, have a blast!

Key Points

- Design space and environment for a specific experience.
- Make choices available.
- Staff members are there to offer choices, provide resources, and respond to decisions that are made by the people.

POWER TO THE PEOPLE

Sheltered workshops are designed to keep people in their seats and follow a specified routine. There is no room for creative exploration, because it might upset the schedule. Even if someone gets involved in an activity, he or she still needs to stop when it is break time or lunchtime. Many programs have schedules that dictate when activities will occur rather than allowing for exploration and organic discovery.

The school of thought for many years was that it was best to set up programs with a daily schedule. Classes and clubs were scheduled throughout the day. People rotated to different activities at specified times. It was often called an adult learning approach, similar to a college schedule. But the system was really implemented to provide structure for the staff. It is easier to track staff performance if you know exactly what they are supposed to be doing during a given time slot. Although the model provided individuals with lots of opportunities to learn and do new and exciting things, it did not allow them to explore their own interests or discover new talents. Although doing science experiments and building towers out of toilet paper rolls may be very cool, those activities do not allow people to develop their own talents and interests.

Giving people permission to explore by not adhering to a schedule can be very powerful. Continuing to build towers because it has turned into a team activity to see who can build the tallest or most creative tower is a good thing. Stopping at 10:00 A.M. and switching to a calculator class disrupts the creative process and minimizes the potential for the experience to evolve. The structure is in place for exploration as opposed to being designed to fit the schedule. Go with what works! Follow the flow and let the people drive the schedule for each day.

Chad Collins is an artist at Creative Foundations in Marysville, Ohio. Creative Foundations is a day program that gives individuals the choice to earn an income while creating art and selling it to the community. They have four locations in central Ohio. Chad describes the difference between his experience in a sheltered workshop and his current day program: "I like it here because I am able to do something I enjoy as opposed to something I don't care for." At the workshop,

Chad working on a giant puppet mask.

(CREATIVE FOUNDATIONS, MARYSVILLE, OHIO)

he worked on an assembly line. He said, "We had the option to change positions on the line, but it was still the same. It got pretty monotonous after a while." Now that Chad has control over his day, he attends "every day, rain or shine." His attendance at the old workshop was not as stellar. He also is making minimum wage, plus a commission for artwork that sells—and Chad sells a lot of artwork.

A lot of the support plans and behavior plans that we develop for people are a response to the symptoms of boredom. It is natural for people to generate their own stimulus. In the absence of positive stimulation, they may begin pinching, poking, and annoying people just to get a reaction. Positive or negative, these behaviors create a connection and evidence of self. In the traditional sheltered workshop, we have designed an environment where people cannot be successful. They are suspended in time. All too often the leadership and staff ultimately just want them to show up, be quiet, and return every day so that the staff members can collect their checks. Chad Collins said that in the workshop he was "rushed to do things, had limited restroom breaks." He continued, "Some of the staff were disingenuous—just there to get a paycheck." This is not a place to celebrate the individual. This is a place that strips people of their individuality and wants them to act like robots: to show up and do what they are told. Wait, work, and be quiet.

Does this seem harsh? What if this were your life? What if you were going to school and finding opportunities, exploring interests, and talking of employment options only suddenly to find that you have transitioned into a "work training center," a system with little regard for your personal interests or potential? As soon as people enter the group mentality with little opportunity to separate themselves from the pack, statistically, they become lifers.

What if you had staff members attend your program for a day? Would they be stimulated, engaged, and excited to be there? Would all of them be good at packaging bolts and heat-sealing plastic bags? Or would they start texting, talking to people sitting next to them, and getting out of their seats? What if we paid them based on how many bolts they packaged? Would they all earn the same wage that they earn as a staff member? Remember, too, that this is an experiment for only one day; it is not their daily life.

Leslie drew and painted the faces onto these funtastic hand puppets.
(CREATIVE FOUNDATIONS, MARYSVILLE, OHIO)

Leslie Rimmer is another artist at Creative Foundations in Marysville, Ohio. Of her former program, she said, “I would get upset at the workshop and cry. I don’t get upset here, because I am happy.” She described her experience at the workshop: “It was noisy. I didn’t like the work. I had to hurry up and eat lunch and then do cleaning work. I didn’t like it, but they wanted me to make more money. They

were pushing me too much to work." After she switched to Creative Foundations, where she had control over her day, her experience was totally different: "It's quiet. I can do my own painting." Leslie is a talented artist who paints beautiful one-of-a-kind flowerpots and can't keep up with demand.

Letting go of a specific schedule actually requires more structure. This is not about creating a free-for-all. We still need to create a safe space for exploration. In essence, we are keeping control of the *who, what* (partially), *when,* and *where* and surrendering the *how.* The *who* is defined by the organization. Who is coming to the program each day? The *what* is defined by the materials and the resources that are provided. The hours of the program determine the *when.* The organization's location determines the *where.* It is *how* the task gets completed that we are releasing. If someone wants to sing a song, we already have the *who* (the person); the essential *what* may be a guitar, drums, piano, or accordion; the *when* is defined by the context of the day. The *where* may be a local coffee shop, a nursing home, or the day program's facility. The person defines the rest of the *what* by determining what instruments to use and what song to sing. He or she also determines the *how* by deciding how the song will be sung.

Creative Foundations has created a safe space for creative exploration. Creative Foundations' studios are all located in downtown storefronts. They provide support to people who want a unique day program experience that focuses on artistic exploration (*who*). They provide a location, materials, resources, and supports (*where, when, what*). The *how* is defined by the individual artists. When Chad Collins decided to make an ice cream cone sculpture for the new ice cream parlor next door, Creative Foundations provided the *who, what, when,* and *where*—Chad provided part of the *what* (I'm going to make an ice cream cone) and the *how* (I'm going to make it out of clay and paint it).

When control shifts to the people, the power struggles go away. Giving people control of their schedule and what they are doing throughout the day naturally elicits buy-in. It is difficult to avoid buying into something that you are creating.

Key Points

- Go with what works.
- Do not be afraid to expand something that is working.
- Shift control from the staff to the people.

COMMUNITY PARTNERSHIPS

Let's make sheltered workshops places where people of all abilities gather to explore and create. Let's make them creative industries, business incubators, an exploratorium. Let's make them the place where people congregate, socialize, and hang out. Let's *be* the community!

The common culture within workshops is to offer substandard programming in a place where most people spend their days watching videos, sleeping, and coloring. This is considered normal, and it attracts money for providing supportive services. But few people in the community ever witness the inside of a program or become familiar with sheltered workshops. Even the annual awards banquet is held outside the workshop. Instead of hiding from the community, we should welcome the community into the program—often! The workshop should be an integral part of the community, a space where people of all abilities can gather. Workshops can be the center of the community! They already have everything they need. They have great free parking, lots of space, lots of restrooms, lots of tables and chairs, and walls on which to display artwork. Many have kitchens, expansive outdoor space, storage areas, and loading docks. Just imagine all of the things that you could do in a workshop if you made it available to the whole community.

Not inviting the entire community to participate leaves gaps. We are missing out. When we use inclusion and cooperation to build partnerships, everyone is more connected. Stories of successful people with disabilities are emotionally potent. Social media explode when people are touched by stories. People love to read the story of a high school football team including and befriending a classmate with Down syndrome. He is their enthusiastic equipment manager and biggest fan. People watch this news report and cry, the family gets interviewed and cries, and the football players become emotional. The equipment manager is excited to be a part of the team. Or read the story of a graduating class electing as homecoming queen a young woman with cerebral palsy and who uses a wheelchair. We feel these stories.

Success stories produce an emotional response from everyone: the person, the family, the media, and the community. When art shows have been installed, floats built, or songs sung, audience members cry and celebrate the talent; the larger and more spectacular the installation or presentation, the more passionate the response. Crafts executed in a less than professional manner may get an "Oh, that is so nice. Those people are busy." Fine art executed so that it carries the spirit of the individual and is presented in a professional and respectful manner takes your breath away. People want to be moved emotionally. They are attracted to opportunities that make them feel good. They want to hear good news, to believe in something better than they thought it could be. The arts can be your vehicle for demonstrating the inherent value of the people you are serving.

We can talk until we are blue in the face about how people need to be part of community. They are just like you and me. Ability First! Concepts are a start, but they do not provide actual opportunities for the community to collaborate. Action begets action. Start doing something. Create the momentum, and you will attract participation. The process of art, also known as making stuff, manifests through the abilities and interests of the artist. It does not take special programming or a special approach. It is the nature of the creative process in every artist. It follows the passion and what works. As artwork is created within a program, the focus moves from disability to evidence of the human spirit. Your program is seen not through the lens of disability but through the vibrant talents and authenticity demonstrated by the individuals. Who is interested in what he or she cannot do? If you are invited to speak at your local Rotary Club and for forty-five minutes talk all about the different disabilities—sensory deficits, cognitive processing challenges, limited mobility—what is this group going to do with this information? Build a playground or install benches?

Imagine same scenario through the Creative Abundance Model. The forty-five-minute presentation to the Rotary Club is full of sharing photographs of people making art; installations in restaurants, libraries, schools, and hospitals; the fabulous float in the Fourth of July parade; collaboration with Master Gardeners; your choir singing at a local nursing home; new garden art sculptures; silver charms designed from drawings; paintings made for the Humane Society's silent auction; and multiple nonprofits fund-raising with donations of your studio's artwork. The picture is now one of a progressive program responding to the opportunities and challenges of the greater community. Your audience is made up of businesspeople involved in a social club organized so that members have the opportunity to network. The key is to create a mutually beneficial relationship. Let people know what you need. Be clear and prepared. Let them know what you can do. Demonstrate a series of successes and speak to how you are an equal partner in business. You are not interested in just receiving donations. You are interested in a lasting partnership. One-time acts of kindness do not sustain a business.

If you ask them to dig a little deeper and design something collaboratively, building on the actual interests and talents of people being served, then everybody learns something new. The group organizes and builds together, encouraging connection within their organization. This is a shift from doing "for," where the people are the recipients of good deeds, to doing "with," where the people are equal partners.

Working with institutes of higher education can also be an opportunity to partner with the community. Many schools offer service-learning opportunities in which students partner with local organizations for a semester of active learning in exchange for college credit. The business school can develop marketing campaigns, facilitate a strategic planning workgroup, or do a financial analysis of a new business venture. And there are many students looking for places to do their internships.

It may feel difficult to establish and maintain a volunteer program. Setting up schedules, finding things for the volunteers to do, and providing training do not always yield a return on the investment. We have found that it is better to ask for something specific from a volunteer, service club, or community organization. For example,

Volunteer and artist Elizabeth Ferrill and artist Bonnie in front of the mural they worked on together. Bonnie ripped pieces of painted paper and Elizabeth hot-glued, forming the puffy white clouds. (COMMUNITY CONNECTIONS, ATHENS, OHIO)

ask Master Gardeners to help people plant a vegetable garden. They will research what plants grow best in the area, make sure the garden gets proper water and light, and lay out the design. That is what they do, and they love it. Ask one of your retired board members to come in once a week and run a scrapbooking club. Ask a nurse to do a first aid class. When volunteers are asked to do something of value that is specific and time-limited, it seems much more appealing.

When you are developing new projects, anticipate the need for volunteer help and how you will ask for it. Inviting community collaboration in each project will create an entrée for participation and will expand opportunities. What if you made a giant Chinese dragon head? It would need five layers of papier-mâché. This would be a great ongoing project to have in the corner of the studio. There would always be something for volunteers and participants to do, and you would get a fabulous, dynamic piece of art to feature in the next parade, festival, or art show or to install at the library.

Key Points

- The program should be the epicenter of the community.
- Collaboration and partnerships are the keys to success.
- Individuals are equal community partners.

CULTURE SHIFT

The Creative Abundance Model delivers both permission and an invitation to the staff. Risk is rewarded. Investigation is the only way to develop new programming. Discovering individual interests is celebrated. Provide the structure and *surrender the process* to the people whose job it is to figure it out.*

The more confident the administrator is with the manager's performance, the less he or she feels the need to control or micromanage. Goals are set, and the administrator leaves the managing to the managers. Confidence allows everyone to embrace more risk and more opportunities for investigation. Subsequently, when staff members have a clear direction and permission to explore materials and ideas, the confidence train chugs through the hearts and minds of everyone. The success of the program is everyone's success! Examine your meetings, systems, and procedures. Determine whether they are a barrier or an asset. Look at your systems to determine whether they are stifling innovation or supporting it. Explore how it could be better. (No more complaining without offering three solutions.)

The urge to control is evidence of fear, and fear will eat up your thoughts and energies. Here is a heads-up: anticipate the best in people but be prepared for jealousies. Yes, this model is about the people, and we all want to create the best services possible. But what happens when a particular area of your program is perceived as a greater success? What if the art area has been in the paper, had a successful show at the community center, developed a product line for the production floor, received a staff award for outstanding community service, and hung artwork in the administrator's office? The

*Thank you, Dr. Lynn Harter, for identifying and describing our approach to programming.

art area seems to subsume the identity of the larger program: "Why are they getting so much attention? All they do is play all day! I've worked here fifteen years and never received an award."

Embrace the Creative Abundance Model across the whole organization and celebrate success together. Without the personal care staff, individuals would not be prepared to work in the studio; bus drivers get people to the program; someone is making sure the lights are on, the building is heated, and the plumbing is working; and someone is putting lunch on the table. It is amazing how much organization and coordination is required so that twelve people can sit around a table and investigate ideas. Remind yourself to thank everyone for creating an environment in which exploration can take place.

The world wants you to be successful. The world wants stories about positive outcomes, stories of personal success, stories of creating beautiful artworks. Getting those stories out into the world can be a challenge, but the real challenge to your growth often lies within your own organization. The naysayers, pooh-poohers, control vampires, eye-rollers, belittlers, and Betty Bullies are the ones who can push the confidence train off the tracks. We suggest that you approach these folks with compassion and love. Negative Nellies are fearful of change. They would hold on to the familiar (even if they are miserable) rather than let go and embrace change. Do not wait to introduce change "after they retire." Remember, the same systems have been in place for thirty-odd years and workers have labored under negative management in factory-like settings. It will take some time for them to believe that if they work differently they will be rewarded. It will take time for them to believe that they can begin to hope, to be excited, and not fear that it will all go away and that the old programming will return. No one wants to be disappointed. People cannot invest in a new model if, in the back of their minds, they believe that it is a fleeting fad.

Another part of the culture shift begins with recognizing that humans are creative beings. We fully come alive when we are creating, making, and doing. If we have experienced only factory-style and janitorial work programs and have not trained or developed respect for our own imaginations, we may believe that repetitive work is the only option possible. Nothing else is imaginable. The only brush that we can use is a toilet brush. Painting could never be someone's work; our limited experience offers no obvious examples. On this treadmill of uninspiring work, we expect the very least, hang on tightly, and never change, while anticipating only a familiar and deadening future. We can jump off this treadmill the moment we decide to. We can change our organizational culture the moment we decide to. If we are familiar with building and creating art out of discarded and repurposed material, we can imagine building it into our programming. We are more comfortable with introducing and sharing things that are familiar.

For example, people not interested in hunting would not want to introduce a hunting component into their programming. They have never hunted. They are not attracted to guns or to killing and gutting animals and eating the meat. These things do not interest them. For others, hunting is at the center of their lives, community, culture, and identity. They derive purpose and partnerships through rites of passage associated with hunting. Staff members within the hunting culture could enthusiastically share this interest with others by developing programs, going on trips, and sitting around a campfire telling stories. That's all well and good for typical people, one might say, but we're talking about the special populations. This is out of bounds! That is true only if you believe it is.

Alaskans spend the warm months filling freezers with salmon, halibut, and moose for the winter. This is their culture. If you are not involved in hunting or fishing, you are on the outside of most conversations, activities, and local goings-on. Hope Community Resources of Kodiak has an accessible boat, and their programming embraces the subsistence lifestyle (a nonmonetary economy that relies on natural resources to provide for basic needs, through hunting, gathering, and subsistence agriculture). It is what is done and familiar. The concept of the agency is to be a support system for individuals to participate fully in their communities. We do not want to reinvent culture; individuals want to be an extension or a part of community and, through creative programming, to even become leaders.

Traditional sheltered workshops have become societies within society, often underutilizing (that is, ignoring) the amazing resources of local culture, networking, and community collaboration. Energies

There is a lot of fishing in Kodiak, Alaska. Hope Community Resources has its own accessible boat, and programming supports people fishing and storing their catch for the winter. Here the boat is being used to gather driftwood to make a bench. (HOPE COMMUNITY RESOURCES, KODIAK, ALASKA)

and resources are directed toward feeding the bureaucratically driven programs. Setting up systems or replicating factory-like settings creates the illusion of control over the individuals supported, whereby everyone is easily supervised or observed. Stepping outside the norm is obvious and can be immediately addressed. Repetitive work is thought of as the answer to all programmatic goals. Compare programs' mission and vision statements with this reality. This type of work is the very antithesis of those high-minded statements. It keeps people from interacting in the community. In today's economy, assembly jobs have all but dried up. If the workshop is supposed to be a training facility with the ultimate goal of transitioning individuals into community-based jobs, few manufacturing jobs exist for them to transition into.

The sheltered workshop and janitorial enclave models tend to offer limited opportunities because the culture of these programs has only limited expectations for the people in them. When we define the potential of another being, we immediately limit opportunity.

For example, the administration and staff of a program may state the belief, "Those people can't run a sewing machine." They cannot imagine folks running a sewing machine, though they have no evidence to prove that the people in their program are unable to do so. In their world, everyone knows that sewing machines are only for staff to operate. If you find yourself imagining the limits of opportunity for a broad group of people, take a minute to ask yourself why. Maybe you will reconsider what you thought to be an absolute rule.

One program we visited has had a sewing component in its workshop for more than thirty years. During this time, people enrolled in the program have made replicable items like table runners, place mats, and bun warmers. Program participants operated the sewing machines and were paid for their work. The workshop then moved from making craft-like items to exploring the creative process and making art. People had been using the sewing machines for years, and there was an expectation that they would continue to operate the machines and generate the products. People were trained to sew, and staff assisted when needed.

The change was not a big deal to the organization, because the type of programming was normal to the administrators. They simply designed a new project that embraced the talents, experience, and equipment used by the individuals and the staff. They collaboratively developed a sewing project with painted fabric. People were not told specifically what to do. Staff members placed a bunch of fabric, paint, wood, and paper on the table. "Dig in!" the participants were told. And the people replied, "We can do what we want?" (This is, after all, what everyone wants to do—what they want.) They saw examples of collaging, incorporating painted fabric, stretching fabric over foam boards to make them easy to paint, and enlarging drawings with an overhead projector. Some people wanted more direction. They were asked to draw and cut out circles (future polka dots) or to hot-glue hundreds of buttons to create an interesting surface texture. People found a place where they were comfortable and enthusiastically jumped in.

Moving from replication to creation was easier for the people than it was for the staff. But with encouragement and support, staff members enthusiastically jumped in and became *very* excited about

the new direction and its limitless possibilities. When shown a bag of samples from other art programs—fabric bunny sculptures, painted pot holders, fancy painted clothing, quilts, and colorful pieces embellished with glitter, buttons, and embroidery—their eyes were opened. Everything was different and unexpected. All of a sudden, the participants ran off to where their personal items were stored and came back with projects they had been working on during their free time, from crocheting and stitching to drawing: amazing stuff! People changed as they shared their personal work. Faces lit up, and people began talking a mile a minute. The feel of the space changed. It was exciting—personal projects were piled on the worktable, covering the workshop products. The lightbulb went on. This would be their new direction. To create a fresh new program within their existing program, all they had to do was use what they already had and think about their resources in a different way. Expanding the sewing and art area made it more interesting to the participants. The work was shared and embraced by the larger community.

As part of such a culture shift, it is important to recognize the difference between art and crafts. How do they differ? Crafts, in the traditional sense, are about replicating a predetermined outcome. The pieces of a project fit together in an expected way, and the participants are just the labor for someone else's idea. When you are working with people with multiple challenges and an angel made of macaroni is the outcome that you are shooting for, not every participant may have the fine motor skills required to replicate the task or the thought processes to lead him or her through the steps of the task. The person's deficits are amplified. And who wants to be reminded of the things he or she is unable to do? With art, you offer someone a pen in anticipation of seeing his or her drawing. Then you respond positively to what is made, understanding that this person is the only one who could make that particular work. Through this simple exchange, you have created an environment where individuals are respected for their personal insight. You have created a platform for discovery, exploration, and experimentation.

As a staff person or facilitator, it is not your responsibility to imagine the completed project. You have the ability to research methods and find materials. You can bring the idea of what process or medium to explore (for example, painting, papier-mâché, quilting, sculpture, doll making, weaving). The content, ideas, and approach to the materials come from your participants. You could say, "This is the correct way to draw a house . . . Everyone follow me." Or you can offer materials and see what happens. Maybe the participants will draw a floor plan or a rabbit hole or a flower. It doesn't matter. In the moment of drawing with someone, you can encourage and ask questions. Point to the drawing and ask, "What happens next?" Encourage the person to expand on his or her idea. Again, you are not responsible in directing the project so tightly that you offer *the* colors for the picture. Ask the participant artists, "What color do you see this giant bunny as?" The question can be asked directly or by holding up a color chart or a few pots of paint. It comes down to listening and responding, respecting the ideas of your participants, and deferring all activity and concepts that can be generated by the participants to the participants themselves.

When staff first learn this method of working and feel uncomfortable, we often hear, "I don't have the time to do one more thing," "I don't like to sing," or "I'm not a dancer." Do not let your fears block new experiences and, in turn, deny exciting opportunities for the people you serve. By participating in something unfamiliar, everyone learns. Doing nothing may be safe, but it is no fun! And no fun makes for a very long workday. Generate fun, and people will be attracted to you and your projects. Fun also attracts attention and energy. We are lucky to work with a group eager to participate and take chances. There is a lot to learn from the people.

Creating institutional change is a series of decisions. You can decide to hold on to what was, or you can decide to try something else. Agencies can be heavy, bureaucratic states in which few are willing to risk standing out. Or the management team may have to vote on all decisions, and they meet only on Wednesdays. Today is Thursday. If they cannot respond to an opportunity until next week, that opportunity may be missed. Be aware of the obstacles that your bureaucracy creates and be prepared to address them by thinking differently.

Key Points

- Celebrate success.
- Embrace the Creative Abundance Model throughout the organization.
- Recognize the inherent creativity in each person.
- Make art, not crafts.

EXPECTATIONS SHIFT

Let's turn sheltered workshops into dream factories—*Charlie and the Chocolate Factory* kinds of factories. If you have someone who loves drawing flowers, enlarge the flower drawings onto cardboard and make them one foot, three feet, or six feet wide. Invite people to paint them beautiful colors and hang them all around the building. Maybe some will be put on stems. Collect some driftwood or 1 × 1 lumber and wrap it with newspaper and tape. Add layers of papier-mâché, paint it, and attach a beautiful flower. Cut flowers out of wood. The next thing you know, you are building a fantasy garden. How about a giant carrot? Collect some cardboard, newspaper, tape, papier-mâché supplies, and paint. Add a little love and *bam!* You have a giant carrot.

When you install pieces throughout your space—in the break room, front office, or main entrance—people start to talk. You hear things like, "How *fun!* How are they doing this? Who is making this stuff? Wouldn't it look great at the coffee shop downtown?" Make one phone call and you have a show at that coffee shop, then a gallery opening where people want to buy the art. Then you start to hear, "How much is it? I want that carrot for my kitchen wall," and "Can they make more?" You figure out a price, and then you need to make more stuff. People are excited, busy, and creating. By exploring and having fun, you have developed something marketable. It becomes about supply and demand. If you make something that people want to buy or that generates attention, you are creating a business opportunity. Whoever thought that the pet rock or sock monkeys would be such huge sellers? Somebody did, and we bought them.

Do you think this is a crazy idea? Could it really happen only within the minds of the authors of this book? No, because this scenario has played out over and over again in programs that embrace the creative process. Artwork often is sold before the paint has a chance to dry. Staff members are off in the corner crying because they see an individual they care so much about painting for the first time. Start to paint wooden chairs, and the next thing you know community members are bringing in chairs and commissioning the artists to paint them. (Don't miss this shift in language: "individuals," "persons served," or "clients" just became and are acknowledged as *artists.*) The local newspaper comes in and does a story about the art, more people commission work, the library wants to book a show, the mayor needs a painted wooden flower to give as an award to the president of the Master Gardener's Club, and Master Gardeners want to buy more flowers. "Can these flowers be installed outside?" Figure that out, and you have a garden sculpture line. The Master Gardeners fall in love with the artists and the program. They start to collaboratively design community green spaces. Connection and networking expand.

All of a sudden, there isn't enough time in the day. You have art to paint, ideas to sketch, galleries to visit. It is a colossal and magnificent shift. It is a lot of hard work and takes energy, but it is fun and exciting. It is very different from the past experience of trying to keep thirty people occupied, people who are disengaged, bored, and inclined to create their own stimulation (poking, pinching, or wandering around). Crisis management or putting out one fire after another is really hard, exhausting work without much joy or positive moments.

But with the shift in expectations, people begin investigating their own interests and designing their own programming. When a staff person says, "This day has flown by!" you know you are on the right track. "I haven't looked at the clock all day! This is the best day we have had in fifteen years!" said one staff member after a day of painting fabric.

Staff often share a common fear: "We can't disrupt the schedule. Randy expects to come in and shred." (There always seems to be a Randy whom everyone believes was born exclusively to shred.)

Flower drawing used as a design to make a large wooden cutout (painted black) with a painted fabric inset, which was installed on a post within the sheltered workshop. We also quilted the stem of the flower, wrapping it with embroidered, painted, and crazy-quilted fabric. (BERKELEY CITIZENS, MONCKS CORNER, SOUTH CAROLINA)

"Randy will have a behavior!" What Randy really likes is to be engaged. Inviting Randy to paint was okay with Randy. The staff members' fear of letting go and seeing what might happen can create an obstacle to his investigation. If Randy does not dig the activity, he can go back to the shredder. He can go back and forth. We must be aware that our fears or predetermined expectations can prevent someone else's opportunity to try something new. What have we got to lose? We cannot even imagine what we have to gain! Opportunity is vast.

Design programming around the anticipation of "behaviors," and you probably will get what you expect. Design programming around the talents and interests of the people, and you probably will alleviate people's need to use their "behaviors" to get what they want. Perhaps Chuck and Doug have had an altercation on the bus on the way to the workshop. But a new painting area and art studio have

Natasha with the collaborative flower installation.

(BERKELEY CITIZENS, MONCKS CORNER, SOUTH CAROLINA)

Diane loves to embroider. Using an embroidery hoop, a shrunken wool sweater (felted), and embroidery floss, she created a work that was the inspiration for and centerpiece of the large painted flower. The flowers and butterfly were installed in the entranceway.
(ACCESSPOINT RI, CRANSTON, RHODE ISLAND)

been set up, and first thing in the morning, people are invited to paint. When there is no boredom, there are no behaviors. This may seem like a very simple approach, one that cannot possibly work. But we have seen it, time after time after time. Chuck and Doug sit side by side all day, working. Staff members are not chasing bored people throughout the building, trying to keep them in their areas, or dealing with "behaviors." People are engaged.

When talking about expectations, it is okay to put your own needs into the mix. If you are going to be a change agent, you must be part of the process. The change must be interesting to you and serve some purpose in your life. You want greater opportunities for your child, brother, friend. You want a more positive work environment. You have been charged with shifting traditional programming into

With a little bit of paint and a lot of love a dull sitting area was transformed into a colorful conversation area. (PIECES OF HEART STUDIO, WILMINGTON, OHIO)

something new. You can imagine a better way, and now is the time to share your vision.

Start making a list. Take a brainstorming approach: no judgment and no criticizing, just a free flow of ideas and dreams, both tangible and nontangible. Use this book as permission to imagine something better. It is not a specific solution to your unique situation. Remember this one principle: programming that is interesting to the people you serve must develop through the interests and talents of the people you serve. You have what you need. Listen, respond, play, invite, build, experiment, enjoy, and be grateful.

Instead of envisioning workshops as assembly lines or factories, envision them as places to assemble ideas. You have a group of people who want to do interesting and engaging things. It is not a problem, it is an opportunity. You have all these people and a space in which to create. If you and they want to design a new product, for example, you have a workforce and an area for production. If you work with community partners, you expand your opportunities.

Design products with the workers' specific qualities in mind, and you will have a customized work opportunity. Take, for example, wooden flower cutouts. They hang on the wall and can become clocks. Screw on a hook for jackets or keys. Turn them into porch decorations, awards, or centerpieces. By designing this product, you combine the interests expressed by the people in the art studio: drawing flowers, painting backgrounds or polka dots, using paint pens and grease markers to add texture. Some people may like to paint in the circles that someone else drew. Combine their talents. If your polka-dot maker starts to draw stripes, that's fine! The special quality of your product line is that no two pieces are exactly the same. If someone wants to draw X's and O's, that's nice. You can share with your customers that those are hugs and kisses. We are attracted to things that make us feel good.

A woman named Margaret loved the X-Men comic books. She loved to talk about them, write about them, and paint about them. She drew X's on everything. When Margaret was in the studio, she painted X's on everything. Her X's gave the artwork an interesting element. Margaret was interested, engaged, and happy. She talked about all kinds of things that morning—her family, her dog, her

Gene Jr. as a "living, breathing painting." Gene Jr. is known for his iconic paintings of houses and villages. Artist in residence Daniel Polnau, inspired by Gene and his work, sculpted a wearable puppet stage. The houses, made of cardboard, are direct translations from Gene's drawings. Gene painted all the houses and insisted that smoke was coming out of every chimney. The end result is an artist collaboration, with Daniel sharing his puppet-making expertise and Gene sharing his iconic image making. The combination is something neither artist could do alone. Through collaboration, a mind-blowing wearable puppet stage emerged. (RESIDENCY WITH COLLABORATIVE ART INTERNATIONAL AND CREATIVE FOUNDATIONS, MARYSVILLE, OHIO)

vacation. After lunch, the agency director came into the studio and said that Margaret was on a behavior plan to not obsess about the X-Men. Oops! We had been embracing Margaret's obsession rather than trying to prevent it. By painting and drawing X's, she was able to use her obsession in a positive way. It also allowed her to open up and talk about other things in her life. Daniel Polnau, a friend of ours who is an artist and puppeteer, often uses the phrase "Work the Quirk." That is certainly another way of looking at it. Don't feel the need to program away people's obsessions. Their obsessions might just be their ticket to a rich, fulfilling life.

When we change our expectations of what is possible, we change the outcome. The community at large is not attracted to a program

that produces pens that are indistinguishable from any other pen you buy at a chain store. They *are* attracted to a program that produces colorful, whimsical artwork that carries the unique qualities of the artists and holds a great, positive story about your community. The sale of art and development of products are not the point. The real point is creating an entrée for your community to become a part of your work. It is about creating the expectation that you have something to share. Your message becomes the celebration of the fabulousness of the artists, their neighbors, and their combined culture and community. We are all connected. If your program is successful, the entire community celebrates because you are of the same place. More quickly than you can imagine, the story will spread, and the celebration will not be contained within your town. It is a human story, a good story, and people will want to share it. People will want to have a piece of the story by visiting and buying art. Your customers will become part of the story. People will want to experience your program, to meet the artists, to see where the art is made. People from other communities may want to replicate the programming in their area. All of this can come about by changing your expectations of what is possible.

ENVIRONMENT

Change the space, change the opportunities. You cannot build an art studio in the old production area as it is set up now, just as you would not ask football players to play on a baseball diamond. But move the tables and chairs into a new configuration that encourages conversation and collaboration, and quickly you will see and feel the shift begin. Arrange the space so that it responds to programming. You can keep moving things until it works. When projects encourage more participation, you simply adjust. Move stuff around again. You will never come up with *the* perfect space design. It will be ever changing. Living things evolve, adapt, and respond, or they die. Your program is a living thing. Responding to new opportunities is growth.

Traditional programs dedicate these spaces to work or to the anticipation of work, even if there has not been any for months or even years. People wait at large tables, ready to pounce on jobs that may never come. They go to break, return to the tables, go to lunch, return to the tables, and then it is time to get on the bus. This ritual is repeated the next day and the next.

As an exercise, list the qualities, approaches, and design of a sheltered workshop. Then imagine the exact opposite.

WORKSHOP: Stations are set up so that people have little opportunity to socialize.

OPPOSITE: Create an area that encourages conversation and the sharing of ideas.

WORKSHOP: People are segregated by skill level to complete a job.

OPPOSITE: Create an area that includes all skill levels, so that people can learn from each other.

WORKSHOP: The space consists of uniform rows of tables with metal folding chairs.

OPPOSITE: Design areas for a purpose: an exercise and dance area without chairs, computer stations, a library, or a music room.

WORKSHOP: Assembly lines are set up with expectations of a specific outcome.

OPPOSITE: Create areas where people can explore materials with the exploration itself as the goal.

WORKSHOP: The floors are made of concrete kept bare and clean.

OPPOSITE: Cover floors with color and paint from a vibrant art studio.

The environment can be made better. Not just a little bit better, but astonishingly better. Ugly factory environments can morph into creative spaces with color, ideas, and connection. You can build new environments through the introduction of an art gallery, a studio, or a music venue. Sheltered workshops are ripe for this type of transformation: they can be redesigned as creative spaces, idea incubators, art studios, or think tanks. They can be a community center, a hub of activity for your local community. They can be a meeting space for local service clubs, a music space for jam sessions, a kitchen space for local food entrepreneurs, or a senior center. They can be a place that nurtures the creative spirit of the people, staff, and community. You already have what you need; you have people, space, and materials. How many times have you seen a commercial warehouse or industrial space turned into something completely different? Your goal is to have a creative space for humans: no more factory-first programming. Let the people work together on projects and respond to community challenges and opportunities.

Preparing a Creative Space

We have encouraged you to encourage others to explore materials and to investigate at their own pace, through their individual interests. You want a happier, more exciting workday for yourself and others. You have decided to embrace the challenge for positive change. Now here are some concrete steps to support your workshop revolution.

Identify an area to become an exploratorium, studio, or idea incubator. Determine how much space you need. The revolution begins with thinking differently. Be curious and open to possibility. The first areas to address are your head and heart—and once they are ready, it's time to jump in. Start by preparing the physical world for the adventure to happen.

Painting/Making Studio—Wet Area

1. Find a space in your building where you can put three 6' × 8' tables together to make a large "quilting bee" setup. Make sure that there is enough room for six to eight people to sit, stand, or work a wheelchair. (Use more or less table space depending on your program and space options. We have found that six to eight people are a good start, and you can always expand once you get your footing.)
2. Set up a paint table near the area where you will store paint, brushes, containers, and rags. It is ideal to be near a sink. If there is no sink presently, see whether there is plumbing access for a sink in the future.

Preparing the area for a new studio.

Paint area ready to go!

Lesley holding up his painting. Fabric was wrapped around blue insulation board and secured with staples. The fabric stays in place, and the boards can be moved around easily.

3. You will need shelving and cabinets for storage. You will fill storage space faster than you can imagine. For example, when people learn that you are collecting lampshades to make giant flowers, you will experience the generosity of your community. Twenty lampshades later, you will be exploring the art of figuring out where they are all going to be stored.
4. The world is full of stuff to paint besides expensive stretched artist canvas: chairs, suitcases, trophies, wood cutouts, fabric, and used hotel bed sheets. To start, pick up three 4' × 8' × ¾" blue or pink insulation board (not the kind that is made up of little white balls that fall apart and fly everywhere). Cut it into 24" × 24" squares, cover with fabric or paper (sheets, old clothes, donated yardage, upholstery material), and staple the covering into place. You can use these boards over and over: when the paint dries, the fabric peels right off. (In contrast, if you use cardboard, the paint adheres to the surface.) You can move these boards around the studio or set them outside;

The foam insulation boards are light and ridged, making them easy to prop up and customize for accessibility. Sissy is painting on old jeans.
(UP AND BEYOND ART STUDIO, HILLSBORO, OHIO)

the fabric stays in place, and you can store and flip through them easily.

5. There can be a lot of anxiety about the floor. If you are introducing this approach, and the vote is to cover the floor, get the largest and best quality tarp you can and cut it down to the dimensions that you want to cover. Tape it down with Gorilla Tape. We prefer working on the floor sans tarp because there is less chance of people tripping or of chairs ripping through the tarp. But if covering the floor is what you have to do, do it. If you can talk others into seeing the area as dedicated studio space, a paint-covered floor becomes evidence of exciting, active programming.
6. You can cover your tables with tarps or go to a mattress store and ask for the discarded plastic the mattresses were shipped in—great stuff!
7. Look for an old-school overhead projector. You can trace drawings onto transparent plastic and project them onto wood, cardboard, or fabric. Then trace the drawings on that surface with a marker, pencil, or paint. Using

Virginia and her bunny drawings. The bunnies were traced onto clear plastic, projected onto two repurposed painted doors using an overhead projector, and outlined. The last photo shows Patty Mitchell and Robert Lockheed with the final installation at a local coffee shop.
(HOPE COMMUNITY RESOURCES, SOLDOTNA, ALASKA)

this approach, a teeny-tiny drawing of a monster can be transformed into a five-foot-tall monster! That is exciting.

8. Create an inviting atmosphere. Hang Christmas lights, encourage natural light (windows), play music, start kooky traditions (for example, at 1:05 everyone sings "Blue Suede Shoes"). Turn this space into a place where the imagination is honored, and be bold about it. This is an idea factory where color, beauty, and experimentation are king!

9. You do not need the most expensive or the cheapest brushes. Gather scholastic-grade, blond, rounded brushes in different sizes and some one-inch and two-inch chip brushes from the hardware store. Try to avoid letting paint dry on the brushes. It will happen, but don't worry: hair conditioner (the cheap stuff) will clean your brushes and save the day. Just rub a little on the stiff brush and voila! (Share this tip with everyone you know; start a save the brushes movement!)

10. For smocks, you can use large business shirts turned around so that they button up the back, hospital gowns, aprons, or large T-shirts. If the sleeves are too long, cut them off! If you cannot button the shirt in the back, wrap yarn around the button and tie it off through the buttonhole. Make what you have work for the activity. Modify it and make it better. Plastic grocery bags over wheelchair controls can be held in place with a rubber band. As your project matures, people will come to work in appropriate clothes or keep painting clothes in their locker to change into.

11. You will need a drying area. Once you have all this great art, it is wet and paint-covered. If your studio is next to a door to the outside, great! Paint dries more quickly in the sunshine. Inside, you can attach a tarp on the wall and on the floor. You will have artwork propped up everywhere throughout the space trying to dry. You do not want the pieces to drip, so they need to dry flat. One of the most fabulous things you can have is a drying rack. We are about making do and building your own stuff, but this is one piece of equipment that is worth buying. A spring-loaded drying rack is a tower that can hold fifty to one hundred pieces of art. The work will not be all over the room or floor, so there will be no safety issue! (Use the safety issue angle when you are negotiating the purchase

Nancy painting. (WASCO, MARIETTA, OHIO)

of a rack.) This is a great item to mention to a local community social club if it asks if there is anything it can do. Racks cost around $1,500 plus shipping.

12. Some of the tools that you will need include a sewing machine, drill, jigsaw, hammer, staple gun, wire cutters, and scissors (some for fabric and others for paper). Fabric scissors are *only* for fabric; they dull quickly if used for paper. You also will need hand-sewing needles, box cutters, and utility knives. Small stuff can be stored in a fishing tackle box. Big stuff fits better in a toolbox that can be locked away safely.

13. Choosing paint is next. Think of paint as color that transforms surfaces. If you are painting fabric that will be an art piece not intended for the washing machine, you can use house paint or tempera or mix them together. Water them down, add sand, or sprinkle glitter over the surface while it is wet, and it will dry into place. If you are painting jeans that will get washed, fabric paint will be a good choice. The more you work with paint, the more comfortable you will become. Some people will want to mix colors or use one at a time or ask for a full rainbow of colors. Some will keep colors bright, while others will mix them until they all become a uniform brown. It is all okay. Exploring the process is the most important part of

the experience. And it is only paint! Besides, you can layer and layer paint until it feels finished. One person draws an image, another wants to paint it in, another adds polka dots, another writes a poem down the side, and someone else cuts out flowers and glues them on. You have an amazing piece of collaborative art.

14. More on paint: house latex paint is great. You can have bright fabulous colors mixed, and it is *much* cheaper than purchasing tubes of acrylic paint. Find the mis-tint section at the paint store and ask whether color could be added to turn a light green into a bold green. *Do not* accept or ask for donations of house paint. You will get stuff that has gone bad, was frozen, has dried out, and otherwise has become nasty. If people see your studio as a great way of getting rid of old paint, it will be more of a hassle than it is ever worth. Buy your house paint. Accept donations of tempera, acrylic, or watercolors but never house paint.

Some programs have tons of space, while others feel cramped. Reimagining and redesigning the space for specific investigations will encourage flow and create a comfortable feeling. People will understand when they are in the painting studio that this is where it is okay to paint. They do not have to worry about the floor or their clothes getting messy (smocks are available). Even better, they begin to come to work in clothes that they know are okay to get paint-covered.

During one residency, we were painting. On day two, one of the staff members said that she had received a call from Samantha's grandmother about paint on her clothes. Oh, no! We had tried to be careful! The workshop had sent out notes saying that we were going to introduce paint: "Please wear clothes that you don't mind getting a little paint on." We were relieved to learn that the grandmother was so excited that she had cried when Samantha came home with paint on her. She must have been participating in a project! Samantha has severe cerebral palsy, uses a wheelchair, and was perceived as someone who could not contribute to an art project. Her grandmother knew better, and so did we. With the help of a couple of clamps to hold the canvas and a plastic glove, Samantha was able to paint beautiful images by blending colors.

What if people are not interested in art? The process of designing the environment for other purposes is no different. You simply have to envision what will be happening in the space and design it accordingly. To set up a space to explore theater, you will need a stage, or a place to move around; boxes of old clothing, hats, and props for improvisation and costumes; a karaoke machine or sound system; and a quiet space for thinking, writing, and creating.

CONTINUOUS EVOLUTION OF DISCOVERY

One workshop developed a live music program. Hours went into finding funding, writing grants, and booking artists. It was great. Community members came in and performed on Fridays; staff liked it; people were into it. After one of the performances, a visiting artist left his guitar out, and a staff member picked it up and started playing really well. "You play?" Some staff had been bending over backward to bring live music into the programming, and all the while, a staff person, working right there in the activity area, was a musician? "Why didn't you tell us you played?" His response: "You didn't ask." Even if you think you are being welcoming and inviting, never assume. Yes, he could have been more forthcoming, but he was not. What kept him from coming forward and sharing his talent and interest?

We are serious about change. Workshops must change, or they will close. The writing is on the wall. Olmstead, Employment First, federal lawsuits, and state mandates are all putting pressure on workshops to close their doors. The message is clear: workshops are not a viable place for people to spend their day. We can do better.

New, responsive, independent day programs are opening up across the country. If they provide attractive programming, people will gravitate to what is more interesting. Would you sign up for services at your facility? If yes, why? If no, why not? Are you providing the services you would want to receive? If you were in a car accident tomorrow and experienced a traumatic brain injury, would your postinjury self be satisfied with the job your preinjury self did in designing and offering programming options?

Is this too dramatic? Not really. It feels more dramatic when you imagine yourself as a person receiving services. You can imagine it, but it is reality for the people enrolled in your agency. Offering quality programming is the right thing to do, and programs are slated for big changes anyway. Across the country, the traditional sheltered workshop model is being challenged. Paying a subminimum wage will not be an option, and contract assembly work is dwindling. If staff and management need motivation to change, maybe this is it. Change and have a job, or fight change and find yourself without a job. We much prefer the positive approach. Times are changing, and we can seize this opportunity to explore and create new exciting workshop spaces. We are grateful to be part of the revolution, and we are motivated to share it with you and with others. It is an exciting and unique moment in history. *You* can help design a new approach.

Taking the time to get to know people is critical. Having intense small-group and one-on-one time really helps you learn a lot about each participant. You may learn that Doug really likes to tell jokes. He is a prankster and loves to make people laugh. Because he was always trying to get a reaction out of people, he had a tendency to grab and poke them. How could you turn what was perceived as a negative into a positive for Doug? Making Doug the center of attention during different times during the day would help him get the reinforcement that he needed. He could tell a knock-knock joke every day at the morning meeting. He could participate in theater activities that would allow him to be the star. What if he honed his talent and went to an open mike night? What if he got a gig on the local radio station telling the joke of the day? If you are responsive and open, the possibilities are endless.

We suggest a creative, organic model. Use the rich abundance that is the people who are attending your workshop. Nobody is told exactly what to do, but they are asked to explore and find what is interesting and what "sticks." For it to work, everyone, especially direct support staff, need to believe in the power of the investigation —to go where it leads them and know that it will always be a moving target. You will not find the solution and be able to replicate one day so it looks like another. "Yes, we tried papier-mâché last week, and the group lost interest by Wednesday." Did the group lose interest, or did the staff—the catalyst for fun—and the team leader lose interest? Did you make little tiny sculptures that were hard to cover with papier-mâché? What if you built a five-foot structure out of 2 × 4's in the form of a deer and then beefed it up with newspaper and tape? If you found sticks that looked like antlers and figured out how to attach them to the head, then added more scrunched-up paper? Hey, it is starting to look like a buck! Tape it really well and add layers of papier-mâché. How can you say that this activity wouldn't be a fun and exciting team learning experience? People would learn team dynamics, building skills, problem solving, and more. The office staff would come back into the workshop to see what everyone was talking about. People would start to have their pictures taken with "Bucky" (he has a name now), and you keep working on it until it is ready to paint. Add big brown eyes and a shiny nose. When finished, Bucky is installed first in the main entrance and then in the visitor's center in town.

Are you done? Is it time to pat each other on the back and declare that is the end of that? Absolutely make some time to celebrate the group's accomplishment. But be aware of what you are celebrating. Are you celebrating the collaboration, a fully realized ambitious project, or your collective creative genius? Remember, this is not the end . . . it is the beginning. This process of making and offering engaging projects never ends. One experience encourages the next. You made Bucky. Now do you make his mate? Or an elephant, dog, cat, tree, rock, a hundred birds? You can make anything you want. You can do anything you want. What you cannot and must not do is sit there and do nothing. You can play the guitar and sing with people and make instruments, costumes, and hats. You can work on a parade entry for six months! Make a thousand flowers out of recycled soda bottles to decorate your float. When asked, "What do you do?" how many people can answer, "Anything I want" and really mean it? We are so lucky to work with fun people, investigating new things. Take full advantage of this opportunity and introduce the things you have always wanted to do.

Investigation of ideas by exploring new materials is not to be confused with being entertained by the introduction of new materials. We are familiar with staff talking about what they are going to do on Monday: "We did paper snowflakes this week. What are we going to do next week? Are we going to hook rugs, paint wooden craft figures,

Artist in residence Daniel Polnau was inspired by Jessie and her beloved elephant Ellie—collaboratively making this large elephant puppet.
(CREATIVE FOUNDATIONS, MARYSVILLE, OHIO)

glue macaroni angels, or make reindeer out of Popsicle sticks?" Their belief is that people can be interested in projects for only so long and that once they have completed a project, they ask, "What's next?" They fear that the staff will be run ragged, looking for entertaining stimuli and feeling responsible for finding the next best activity. Finding things that the entire group will be interested in doing for two hours until the bus comes, that are accessible for all skill levels, and that can be completed in the designated time is exhausting work.

"I want to make a clown wearing a crab hat." Cool! Puppeteer Daniel Polnau and Jessica worked on this fantastic collaboration. (CREATIVE FOUNDATIONS, MARYSVILLE, OHIO)

At a studio in Ohio, artists started a project, first painting fabric and then combining the work into an 8' × 12' mural that was installed at the entrance of their building. But they were not "finished." They were excited about what was next, continuing to investigate painted fabric and sewing. They had experience with these media, and this familiarity allowed their ideas to manifest fluidly. They began the process not as novices but as experienced sewers. Their years of practice, working with fabric and using sewing machines, created a broad skill set, and they were able to translate those skills into this new creative endeavor. Making things is a combination of study, repetition, and practice—becoming familiar with the characteristics of your material. The more comfortable, familiar, or expert you become with your medium, the better you will be able to transform ideas into the physical world.

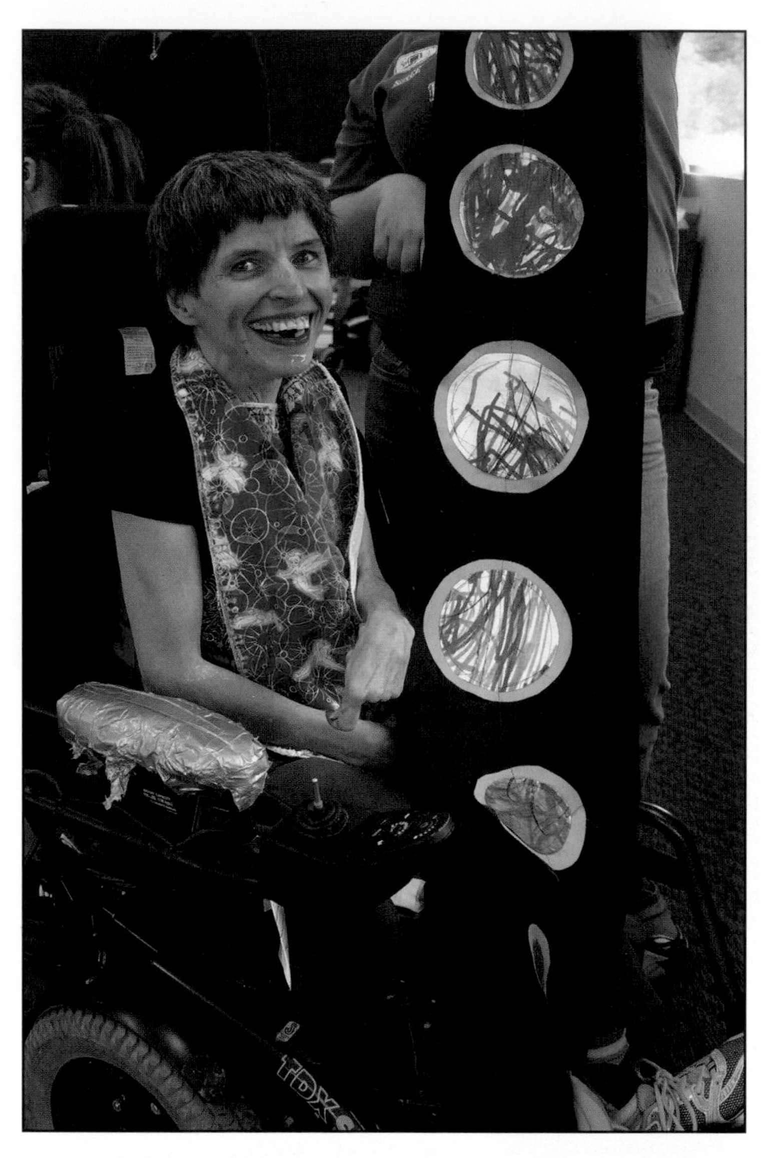

Jeannie's drawings on fabric were cut out as circles and sewn onto black fabric. Additional decorated fabric was cut out in the shape of a drawing by Carolyn, and everything was sewn together by artists in residence Wendy Minor-Viny and Patty Mitchell (author). (COMMUNITY CONNECTIONS, ATHENS, OHIO)

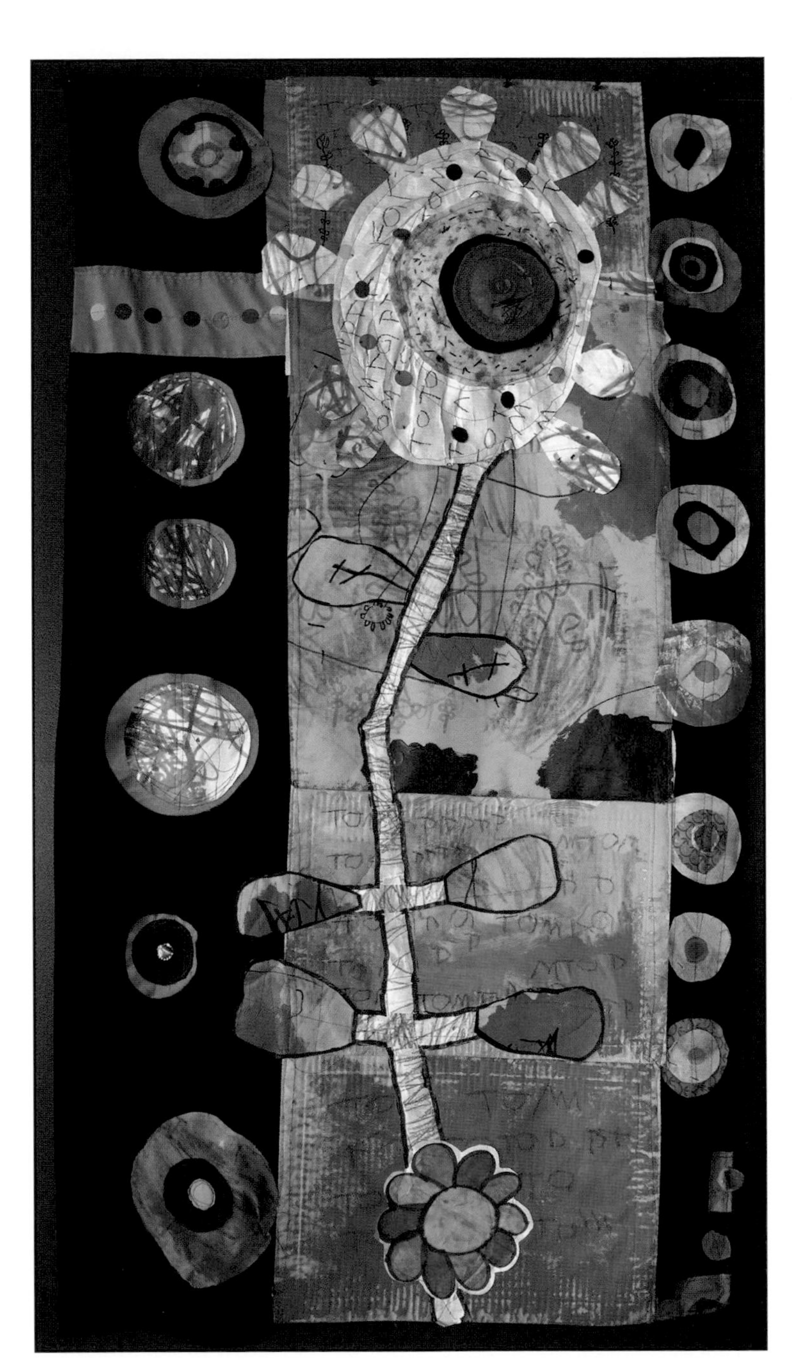

Think of something that you are familiar with, like driving a car. Remember when you were first behind the wheel? You had been riding in cars your whole life, but this was different. Having been a passenger, you were familiar with the car, roads, and riding at sixty-five miles an hour, but you were not the driver. The excitement, discomfort, responsibility, and freedom were about to become yours! It required practice with checking mirrors, turning the key, releasing the brake, and putting the transmission in drive. There was a system, and you had to go consciously through the steps. After twenty years of driving, you are still going through those same steps, but now they are second nature. The same principle applies to playing sports. The novice Ping-Pong player approaches the ball awkwardly. The experienced player is fluid and responsive: there is muscle memory, familiarity with the paddle and table, and awareness of strengths and weaknesses. Or think about cooking. Your boss says that you have to serve a dinner for six next week. This could be a dream come true or a nightmare. It all depends on your experience and interest.

The artists have been working with painted fabric and sewing for years now, and they never have made the same thing twice. Find materials that are interesting to you, and stay with it. It is the investigation that is interesting. You may make painted fabric murals just to see where that process takes you, and then one day someone wants to make a project that is more sculptural. That's great! You do not have to reinvent yourself and gather new materials to make that happen. You have everything you need. You just have to learn about taking a two-dimensional piece of fabric and making it three-dimensional. Take apart a stuffed animal. How did they shape the head? Replicate what you see and experiment. What if you do not have stuffing? Do you have newspaper, plastic bags, and scraps of fabric? Use what you have, and keep going. Build that bunny!

The continuation of programming is like making a pot of coffee. If you desire a hot, delicious, flavorful cup of delight, get your elements together. You make and share the coffee with your friends. You drink your way through the first pot and decide you need more. It worked so well the first time that you pour more water into the coffee maker, expecting exactly the same outcome. But it is not the same outcome; it is a watered-down version of the previous experience. You say, "I did exactly the same thing but didn't get the same outcome."

But the situation had changed. By adding fresh coffee grounds to the mix, you again have a satisfying experience.

The point is that you cannot do the exact same thing over and over and think that people will stay engaged. You can build with the same materials (wood, cardboard, and fabric), but you must anticipate and respond to new ideas and expand your approach to the material that you have become familiar with. Placing materials on a table and walking away is not programming. Some people may appreciate the opportunity to explore on their own. But for many others, your participation, enthusiasm, and sharing the experience of investigation may be at the core of programming. A pool table is not programming. How staff members interact with individuals using the table is programming. The table is just a vehicle for interaction.

We often hear, "It is great when it works. I like hearing these stories, but how do I know this will work for my program? The unknown makes me uncomfortable." Well, why do people ride roller coasters? Fear and excitement are cousins.

The more you do, the easier it will become. We promise. It is like a giant snowball rolling down a mountain. As it grows and grows, rocks and trees stick to it, and the momentum increases. It started out as a little snowball, but energy and activity are attractive. You will encourage enthusiasm if *you* are enthusiastic, exploration if *you* explore, dancing if *you* dance, and writing if *you* write. The possibilities are endless.

This approach may seem overwhelming. Just break it down into sections. Nothing begins at the end. You have to work through the process, and that is the fun part. And if you do play the guitar, bring it in to work and play for people. If you play golf, bring your putter in and give a putting lesson. You will be doing something that you love, and the individuals will totally dig it.

Examine why you are holding back or afraid. Pay attention to your feelings, breathe deeply, and push through it. Be brave.

Key Points

- The process itself may be the outcome.
- Believe in the power of investigation.
- The way we deliver services is changing, and we must be prepared to respond to new expectations.

THE NATURE OF ATTRACTION

In the past, programs have been seen as charities. Community members and groups wanting to do good would extend a helping hand: "Oh, those poor people!" It was not a partnership. These exchanges were motivated by pity and enacted at the whim of the entity perceived to be in the power position. Donating money and clothing and participating in an agency picnic are one-time experiences, allowing community members to say, "I did my part." But those community members were not drawn to the program for a mutual experience.

When there is an actual exchange between parties, one in which each benefits from the other, there is an increased chance of an expanded relationship. A person paints a flowerpot that is kind of messy and not well executed. But it costs only a dollar, and buying it would be a nice thing to do, so you buy it. As a consumer, would you return and buy other pieces and tell your friends about the experience? Can the individual really build a business with such a limited and perhaps nonexistent profit margin? Art made by anyone, disabled or not, must possess an attractive quality in order to develop an appreciative market.

If you consider yourself a charity, you will be one. If you think of yourself as a community partner, you will find ways to benefit the people and the greater community. Make jewelry and sell it in a local shop. If the shop owner is doing this as a favor and not receiving any financial gain, it is not fair to imagine the continuation of this opportunity. It may be costing that shop owner space, staff time, and sales to host your pieces. Customers may be buying your product and not buying other merchandise in the shop. If you think of yourself as a business partner and establish a wholesale price, the shop owner sees you like any other business and will not have a reason to end the relationship. It is in an agency's best interest to be a good partner and to enter into mutually beneficial business partnerships.

Some programs have tempered growth and self-reliance because they do not want to jeopardize traditional funding streams. They believe that dependency will encourage continuation of present funding streams. Imagine a situation in which the administration actively worked to stop the growth of an art studio while preserving and investing in a failing recycling business. What kept the administration from responding to a growth opportunity? Perhaps it was fear of success. The success of a studio should be viewed as a solution, not a problem.

The agency's belief system sets the stage for its success or failure. It should be agreed that every person possesses an individual genius. People receiving services are the experts in developing their own programming. The abilities and interests of staff and participants make up a unique blend and create opportunity for programming. What you believe, what you imagine will manifest. We attract the things that we want by being open to the opportunity. If we bury our heads in the sand and shut our eyes to the opportunity, we will never grow.

"These people will never make anything that anyone would want to buy." If you believe this, why would you ever investigate their talent and artistic creativity? If you believe that the best we can do for people is to give them a safe place, away from the greater community, and that it does not matter how people spend their days (for example, with coloring books and puzzles or stringing beads), then "whatever" is good enough. Whatever becomes reality.

If you believe that programs can be a means to combine enthusiastic people, space, and time by transforming communities and developing business opportunities, partnerships, and interaction with higher education, then you will find those opportunities and will attract people to your program as active partners.

Key Points

- Think like the businesses and people that you want to partner with.
- Quality programming and quality products create quality outcomes.

SHARE THE ABUNDANCE

This process does not ask agencies to reinvent the wheel but instead encourages them to develop relationships and partnerships. No business operates as a solo entity. There is always an interdependence:

Jenny's drawing of a fireweed used in the design of a pendant and the studio's logo. (HOPE STUDIOS, ANCHORAGE, ALASKA)

Hand-painted fabric made into a tote bag. (SOARING ARTS STUDIO, NAPOLEON, OHIO)

Elaine with dog leashes and fluffy visitor. (HOPE STUDIOS, ANCHORAGE, ALASKA)

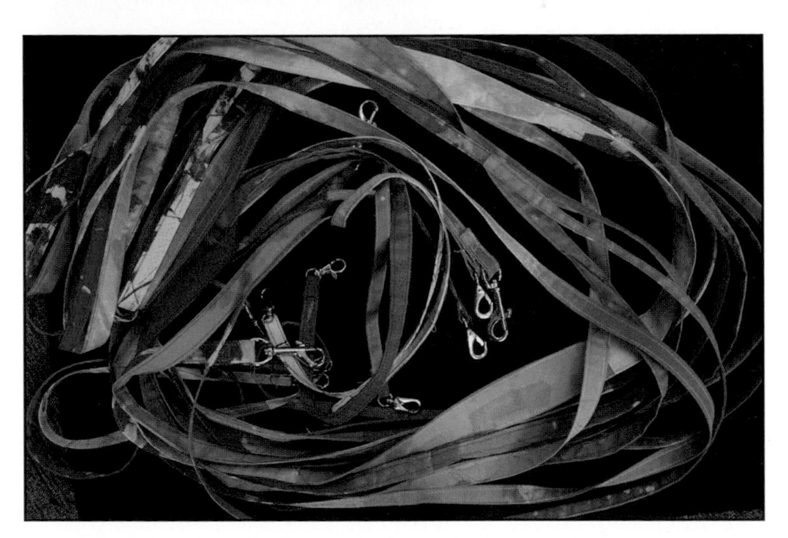

Painted sturdy fabric made into dog leashes. (HOPE STUDIOS, ANCHORAGE, ALASKA)

shipping systems, raw materials, marketing streams, customer bases . . . The list is extensive. Sheltered workshops have operated as isolated communities within a community. Their vision is limited, and they cling to a scarcity model that promotes a fear-based culture. But when the view is widened past the front doors, down Main Street and beyond, then opportunity expands, and the abundance model can be embraced.

In the same vein, your future successes should be shared. "When you share, you double the joy." The more you do and share with the world, the more will come back to you. There is a human tendency to think, "This is my idea," and to be protective, secretive, and exclusive. We do not want other programs to do what we do, steal our ideas, and know our secrets. We do not want to put our story on Facebook, because "they" will see what we are doing. When staff members claim something as theirs, others worry that they are stepping on toes and trespassing across invisible lines.

No living person invented painting, sculpture, or whatever else you are doing. Everyone has been inspired by someone or something else. If a project you are working on encourages a different agency to make stuff, great! Don't say, "Oh, but they are our competition. We shouldn't share with them!" The point of agencies is to be a support system for people with developmental challenges. If people have choices in where they go for programming, it is a good thing. Different programs will offer different choices, such as health and exercise, doggy daycare, or gardening, and they will attract different people. If you are great at what you do, you don't have to worry. Put your energies into developing fantastic programming.

If you believe that ideas and resources are scarce and limited, you will focus on what you do not have. If you believe that ideas and approaches are limitless and constantly expanding, then you will focus on the abundance that is all around you. This is the heart of the Creative Abundance Model!

What if you had a stash of material (like silk) and you protected it? You did not use it in your sewing, because you did not want to let go of something that was so precious. It just sat there. You looked at it and used other fabrics in your projects. Then one day, you decide to sew some of the silk into a quilt. Friends see your quilt and say, "Oh, I didn't know you used silk. I have some I'll never use. Do you want it?" And the next thing you know, people are giving you their old silk shirts. One friend makes sure that when she travels to Thailand, she brings back some silk for you. By letting go and sharing, suddenly you have unlimited access to what you held precious.

A studio started doing projects with dryer lint. They rolled the lint and glue into little balls to make beads, which they then used to make earrings. It was funny and a little goofy, and the earrings were really pretty. The story started getting around the community, and people began bringing in dryer lint for them. Before they knew it, they had bags and bags of the stuff! Dryer lint is abundant, and people are willing to share!

Programs that are transparent and public and that share ideas grow at an astounding rate. Programs that protect their ideas and build an insular culture do not expand and are not as successful.

When we do public presentations and share our approaches, we ask that programs in turn build a culture of sharing. We share with you, you share with others. Keep the love going. We have two Facebook pages (ART THINK TANK, INNOVATION THINK TANK) that invite people to post ideas, questions, and projects that they are working on. Sometimes people ask, "Aren't you afraid that if everyone introduces the arts into programming it will all look the same?" If we do a project with Main Street Beautification, should we worry that someone else will want to copy it? We are not worried at all, because every program is different. They all have different people, approaches, resources, and community partners. The more studios that are established in workshop settings and the more workshops that evolve into community centers, the fewer workshop doors will close and leave people with even less opportunity for programming. The more familiar the public becomes with the concept, the greater the community collaborations will become. Some may say, "We don't need an art studio; they have one in the next county." Good for them. But does it benefit anyone in your program if people elsewhere are getting the chance to explore? Go visit the other program, become partners, make collaborative art projects, Skype, or do an art show together.

Pieces of Heart is a studio in Wilmington, Ohio, that has been making great stuff. They painted their furniture, painted the walls bright blue, made wooden cutouts, sewed, and created fabric arts. They started selling the artwork by auctioning a piece of work through their affiliated thrift store. Then they had a wildly successful gallery show at the local college, totally rockin' it. A workshop in neighboring Hillsboro was introducing a similar programming style. The Hillsboro staff member identified to run the arts program visited Wilmington's program. She got to be inside an active studio, see the individuals working and engaged, learn how the space was organized, and ask questions. The concept of a studio space became less mysterious to her, and the two art staffers bonded and are now allies. Up and Beyond Studio was totally kickin' in Hillsboro after just a few short months. They were able to ramp up faster, price their artwork faster, and make sales faster by learning from the Pieces of Heart Studio. The two programs are stronger and more vibrant because of their connection. Sharing expanded possibilities has made both programs more successful.

You can share examples of success from other programs with your board members, staff, participants, and families. This approach is no longer a theoretical concept. Amazing opportunities are possible with a shift in thinking and attitude. There is *no* limit to what we can do through the creative process. Ideas and opportunities expand. Implement, improve, and share!

Find examples at www.NorwichCS.com and www.CollaborativeARTInternational.com.

Key Points

- You do not have to reinvent the wheel.
- Focus on the abundance around you.
- Share ideas with others to increase opportunities for your own organization.

WHAT WE HAVE LEARNED

THIS IS no longer business as usual.

BUILD THAT BUNNY!

Share what you know.

LET GO!

Celebrate success.

COLLABORATE!

Move your organization from the shadows into the light.

HAVE FUN!

Dale and Susan Dlouhy.
(UP AND BEYOND ART STUDIO, HILLSBORO, OHIO)

Jean and Patty Mitchell.
(HOPE COMMUNITY RESOURCES, KODIAK, ALASKA)

meet the authors

SUSAN DLOUHY

Susan Dlouhy has worked for thirty years in a variety of administrative roles supporting people with disabilities. She was the director of two sheltered workshops in Ohio in the 1980s, 1990s, and 2000. She worked as the administrator for a statewide association for twelve years, where she developed training and provided technical assistance to sheltered workshops across Ohio.

Ms. Dlouhy is now the president of Norwich Consulting Services, where she works with organizations to transform their programming from the sheltered employment model to the Creative Abundance Model. She also consults with organizations in the areas of leadership development, strategic planning, and program design. As an independent consultant, Ms. Dlouhy has written and administered grants for the Ohio Rehabilitation Services Commission and Ohio Developmental Disabilities Council. Ms. Dlouhy obtained her master's degree in rehabilitation counseling from the Ohio State University. She is a certified rehabilitation counselor and licensed professional counselor.

PATTY MITCHELL

Patty Mitchell is an artist and social innovator specializing in collaborations between artists with and without perceived differences. Her dream is turning sheltered workshops into creative spaces.

As an artist in residence, Patty Mitchell has helped organizations nationally and internationally start up arts programming ventures. Some examples include Our Town Studios, Flor de Arte, Soaring Arts Studio, Passion Works Studio, Pieces of Heart Studio, Up and

Beyond Art Studio, Hope Studios, Kudos Studio, Kan Du Studio, Colores del Alma, Just Imagine Studio, and AccessPoint RI.

Ms. Mitchell has received a Distinguished Alumna Award from Ohio University's College of Fine Arts, an Ohioana Citation for Art and Education, an Individual Artist Award from the Ohio Arts Council, a Citizen of the Year Award from Civitan, and the Keystone Award from Ohio University for outstanding community service. Patty Mitchell received her BFA and MFA from Ohio University's Fine Art Photography program.

CONTACT INFORMATION

SUSAN DLOUHY

Website: www.NorwichCS.com
E-mail: susan@norwichcs.com
Facebook: Norwich Consulting Services
Twitter: NorwichCS
LinkedIn: Norwich Consulting Services

PATTY MITCHELL

Website: www.CollaborativeARTInternational.com
E-mail: patty@collaborativeartinternational.com
Facebook: Collaborative Art International